THE PIP ANTHOLOGY OF WORLD POETRY
OF THE 20TH CENTURY
VOLUME 3

GREEN INTEGER
6022 Wilshire Boulevard, Suite 200A
Los Angeles, California 90036

(323) 857-1115 fax: (323) 857-0143
E-Mail: lilycat@sbcglobal.net
visit our web-site: www.greeninteger.com

THE PIP

ANTHOLOGY OF WORLD POETRY
OF THE 20TH CENTURY

VOLUME 3

Edited by Régis Bonvicino, Michael Palmer and Nelson Ascher
With a Foreword by João Almino
Revised with a Note by Douglas Messerli

EL-E-PHANT 3

GREEN INTEGER
KØBENHAVN *&* LOS ANGELES
2003

GREEN INTEGER BOOKS
Edited by Per Bregne
København/Los Angeles

Distributed in the United States by Consortium Book
Sales and Distribution, 1045 Westgate Drive, Suite 90
Saint Paul, Minnesota 55114-1065

(323) 857-1115/http://www.greeninteger.com

First Green Integer / EL-E-PHANT edition published 2003
English language translations and revisions
Copyright ©1997 by Sun & Moon Press
for the translators and editors.
Revisions and new material ©2003 by Green Integer.
A slightly different edition of this book was
first published as *Nothing the Sun Could Not Explain:
20 Contemporary Brazilian Poets* (Los Angeles:
Sun & Moon Press, 1997)

This book was made possible, in part, through a matching
grant from the Foreign Ministry of Brazil
and the Consulate General of Brazil in San Francisco.

Typography: Kim Silva
Photographs: first row—Horácio Costa [Regina Stella]; Régis Bonvicino [Vladimir Fontes];
Claudia Roquette-Pinto [Vladimir Fontes]; second row—Duda Machado [Vladimir Fontes];
drawing of Paulo Leminski; Francisco Alvim [Aldolfo Montejo Navas]; third row—
Carlito Azevedo [Vladimir Fontes]; Arnaldo Antunes; Ana Cristina Cesar.

LIBRARY OF CONGRESS CATALOGING IN PUBLICATION DATA
Régis Bonvicino [1955] Michael Palmer [1943], and
Nelson Ascher [1958] eds. ; revised by
Douglas Messerli [1947]
*The PIP Anthology of World Poetry
of the 20th Century*
Volume 3:
*Nothing the Sun Could Not Explain—
20 Contemporary Brazilian Poets*
p. cm — Green Integer / EL-E-PHANT 3
ISBN: 1-931243-04-2
I. Title II. Series III. Translators

TABLE OF CONTENTS

A NOTE

When, in the year 2000, the Sun & Moon publication of *Nothing the Sun Could Not Explain* sold out its first printing, I felt it was necessary to reprint the title. But in the interim I had begun *The Project for Innovative Poetry Series of World Poetry of the 20th Century*, and it immediately became apparent that this volume would be a perfect fit in that series. Although most volumes were determinedly random in their selections, I also felt it important to organize some of the projected 50 volumes around aesthetic, regional and national selections.

However, as Régis Bonvicino, friend and primary force behind the original volume, had pointed out, there were a few errors to be corrected. Moreover, the older volume would have to be reformatted, with larger biographies and complete lists of titles, in order to bring it into the style of the PIP series. As I began the complex process of rewriting biographies and obtaining publication information, it also quickly became apparent that there was a larger number of editorial errors and inconsistencies in the original volume than we had suspected. Many of these problems were inevitable, given that the editors and translators were working in two different countries across two continents. A few were problems of form and intentions of the earlier volume.

As I began to make these corrections, I also perceived that this was a perfect time to bring the earlier volume up to date by adding some new poems and translations that had appeared since our original publication (chosen primarily from the selection in *New American Writing* titled "Lies About the Truth: An Anthology of Brazilian Poetry," edited by Régis Bonvicino in collaboration with Tarso M. de Melo) and to reconsider a few of our earlier choices. In the end we added a substantial number of poems, dropped one of the original poets and added another, a young Brazilian writer from the Amazon rain forest, Antônio Moura.

The process of reediting took longer, I believe, than anyone expected; but in the end it has greatly improved the quality and breadth of the original publication. As with all such publishing and editing, there are a great number of people to thank. In particular, Régis Bonvicino worked energetically to provide me with new information and was, at all times, the great supporter of this new version. Michael Palmer and Nelson Ascher must also be thanked again for their original editing, as well as João Almino for his Foreword and his original support of this project. Similarly, Ambassador José August Lindgren Alves of the Consulate General of Brazil in San Francisco must be thanked for his support and patient waiting for the final product. My senior editor, Diana Daves, continues to amaze me with her ever-present commitment to good editing and to publications as free of typographical errors as possible. Intern Alyson Sena worked on this manuscript as well as many others during her long period of involvement with Green Integer. Kim Silva, our typographer, had the formidable task of combining materials from the original text and several other versions—all in different formats. And then there are the many others whose support of this and other PIP anthologies has helped to make the volumes possible: David Antin, Guy Bennett, Rick Gilbert, Paul Hoover, Marjorie Perloff, Jerry Rothenberg, and Paul Vangelisti.

Finally, but not at all least, this volume would have been impossible without the hard work and help of all its translators and linguistic collaborators: Regina Alfarano, Thomas Colchie, Robert Creeley, Jennifer Sarah Frota, Martha Black Jordan, John Milton, Dana Stevens, Michael Palmer, and Charles Perrone.

—DOUGLAS MESSERLI

FOREWORD

The publication of this anthology fills an important gap. In fact, very few anthologies of Brazilian poetry have been published in the U.S. Among them, one should particularly note those which resulted from the initiative of Elizabeth Bishop, Emanuel Brasil and William Jay Smith. These anthologies are, nevertheless, limited to poetry composed prior to the 1970s. Names such as Ferreira Gullar, Mario Faustino and the brothers Haroldo and Augusto de Campos are some of the youngest included in these previous selections.

It is my hope that the publication of this anthology will help increase the interest in Brazilian poetry in the United States and will open the gates to complementary projects. Subsequent anthologies are not only possible but indeed necessary, due to the diversity and comprehensiveness of contemporary Brazilian poetry. A similar potential exists in prose writing as well. In fact, the Portuguese language is spoken by some 200 million people world wide (which is more than French), and its highest literary expressions deserve a stronger presence in English translation.

The present selection starts where the previous anthologies stopped, with names associated with the tropicalist and post-tropicalist movement of the second half of the sixties, and covers other trends in Brazilian poetry since then.

To understand better the cultural context of the younger generations here represented, one should highlight two reference points—one far in the past, the other more recent—regarding the tradition they received.

One is the major reference point for the whole of Brazilian poetry during this century: modernism. Launched at the "Modern Art Week" during the politically turbulent year of 1922, it expressed, through the works of Mário de Andrade, Manuel Bandeira and Oswald de Andrade, among others, a rebellion against parnassian and symbolist movements, liberated the colloquial language, broke with the rigidities of metrics and rhyme and valued, often with wit and humor, the experience of daily life. It opened the gates for a vast spectrum of poetic expressions which included the oneiric images of Murilo Mendes, the mystical illuminations of Jorge de Lima, the metaphysical poetry of Cecília Meireles, the lyrical work of Vinicius de Moraes and the momumental and varied oeuvre of Carlos Drummond de Andrade.

In 1945, at the end of the Getúlio Vargas era (which had started with the 1930 Revolution and had included, since 1937, eight years of dictatorship) and at a time known for the reaction of some poets to the extremes of modernism, João Cabral de Melo Neto's poetry emerged as a unique neo-modernist expression which was anti-lyrical and concerned with form, conciseness and precision. An engineer or architect of language, he is generally considered the most important poet of this period in Brazil.

Cabral de Melo Neto is one of the three great masters of Brazilian poetry throughout this century. Another is Manuel Bandeira, one of the participants of the Movement of 1922, who wrote a poetry of personal memoir, directed toward the small object of daily life. Finally, there is Carlos Drummond de Andrade, a poet whose work endured through several decades, covering a great spectrum of themes related to the subject of the modern man and his world.

As I first intimated, there is a more immediate reference point, either positive or negative, for the younger generations of poets represented in the present selection: it is "concretism," a vanguard movement initiated in the mid-fifties, at a time of great industrial acceleration and technological development in Brazil. One can certainly build a bridge between the objectivity and visual imagery of Cabral de Melo Neto's poetry and the concrete movement, which put new technological resources at the service of poetry and its visual impact. It should, however, be viewed as re-establishing a dialogue with the more radical modernism of 1922, against what was considered a semi-classicist and estheticist rigidity of the generation of '45. It postulates a rupture from narrative and the disappearance of the "self," and favors an atomized poetry across a graphic and visual surface. Concretism projected itself with a great assurance and vitalism across both the national and international cultural stages. The movement, which initially counted in its ranks the poet Ferreira Gullar (who later launched neo-concretism) and which at some point in time encompassed works of other poets, such as José Paulo Paes, had as leaders and most faithful representatives poets Haroldo de Campos, his brother Augusto de Campos and Décio Pignatari. In addition, the Brazilian concrete movement was also important for the visual arts, as witnessed in the works of Mira Schendel, Lygia Clark and Hélio Oiticica.

The present selection starts with the generation following that of the concrete poets. This does not imply that those poets have ceased to work. They have entered a dialogue with the new generation, and their work continues, through its own dynamics, to undergo important transformations.

Due to the criteria employed for the present selection, which is limited to twenty poets and bascially covers poets who are today between 30 and 50 years old, a few important poets not included in previous U.S. anthologies have also not been included in this one (José Paulo Paes, Sebastião Uchoa Leite, Adélia Prado, Orides Fontela, Hilda Hilst, Armando Freitas Filho, among others). Nevertheless, this anthology is highly representative of what has been produced in Brazil throughout the last twenty years, a period during which the country witnessed, in the mid-eighties, the transition from a military regime to a civil government.

The military regime which took power in 1964 and radicalized its authoritarian rule in 1968 is at the origin of the birth of a cultural generation essentially exiled in its own country. In the mid-sixties, the new poets are influenced by the musical outburst of Tropicalism, mainly in Bahia and around the musician Caetano Veloso. A less immediate but still important reference point for them is *Cinema Novo,* whose leading figure is Gláuber Rocha. Even though they maintained a dialogue with the concrete vanguard, they did not follow its rational and apollonian directives. Instead they fashion an informal poetry, marked by disenchantment with the present and lack of confidence in the future, where there is a place for nonrational expression. Their anarchic criticism targets not only the military regime but also the traditional or partisan left, reflecting the lack of closure of their poetry and their disbelief in the possibility of revolution. They are fundamentally concerned with the "here and now." In their use of colloquial language and their subversion of "good behavior," they view their movement as close or faithful to the spirit of modernism of the twenties. Of this group of poets, four are included in the present selection: Torquato Neto, a founder of Tropicalism, and Paulo Leminski, both of whom died young, and Waly Salomão and Duda Machado, both from Bahia, whose work has evolved throughout the years.

In the seventies, encompassing different tendencies which were at the origin of the work of several poets in the present selection and which again evoke the spirit of 1922, poetry offered an aesthetic and critical reaction to political repression. In those days, many poets did not reach their public through the publishing houses. Poets would produce their own books in mimeographed form and would sell them on their own, often in bars and cafés. Their poetry expressed skepticism and an atmosphere of suffocation. Yet to this atmosphere the poets often reacted not by revolt, but by indifference; not with anger, but with humor and irony; not with any programmatic commitment, but with anarchic criticism.

A clearer, if nonsystematic, rejection of the technique of the vanguards occurs, mainly in Rio, with the so-called "marginal" or "alternative" poetry. In a colloquial and informal poetry of immediate experience, life and poetry are often considered one and the same thing. A major reference for this movement is the anthology organized by Heloisa Buarque de Holanda, *26 Poetas Hoje,* which would translate as *26 Poets Today,* published in 1976, and which included poems by Francisco Alvim, Antonio Carlos de Brito (Cacaso) and Ana Cristina Cesar, as well as some of the poets of the tropicalist movement, such as Torquato Neto and Waly Salomão. A well-known poet from Rio de Janeiro not in that selection, but who deserves mention as close to this group, is Armando Freitas Filho. The present selection includes contributions from two of the country's most expressive poets of this movement, Francisco Alvim, whose work has survived these turbulent times, and Ana Cristina Cesar, a poet who left behind a consistent and important work when she committed suicide in 1983, at the age of 31.

Nevertheless, the anthology's main emphasis is on the generation which could be called, for lack of a better word, "post-Concrete," a broad term which pays tribute to the importance Concretism has had in Brazil, mainly in São Paulo through the works of Haroldo de Campos, Augusto de Campos and Décio Pignatari, and includes the establishment of new parameters both in theory and in the poetic tradition.

When I say "post-Concretism," I do not imply that these poets still work within the horizons of concretism. In fact, two among the best poets in this group, Régis Bonvicino and Duda Machado, for example, not only do not consider themselves affiliated with concretism but have ideologically broken with it. Even the most prominent originator of concretism in Brazil, Haroldo de Campos, has long departed from it. Still, concretism has been a major point of reference for this so-called "post-Concretist" generation, which has dealt with a language experimentation whose origin can be found not only in the "concrete" poets, but also in Murilo Mendes, Drummond de Andrade and Cabral de Melo Neto.

With the process of democratization, there has been a broadening of perspectives without any clear cartography. Accordingly, in this anthology, there is a heterogeneous expression both in form and content. Some poems explore a mythic urban world, some a space of intimacy. An important characteristic of many of them is conciseness and a focus on the word as a thing. There are at least two examples of a visual poetry concerned with new media: Arnaldo Antunes and Lenora de Barros. Distinct from this approach, the synthesis produced by the poems of Josely Vianna Baptista, rather than structuring itself out of visuality, parodies it. In the case of Horácio Costa, who lived for a long while in Mexico and is an important translator of poetry from Spanish, the influence of the Spanish-American tradition is evident.

Poets such as Júlio Castañon Guimarães, who is also a keen essayist, Carlos Ávila and Age de Carvalho are all highly representative of the new Brazilian poetry. And the vitality of this generation has been carried forward by the very new voices, as attested to in the poetry not only of Carlito Azevedo, but also Angela de Campos, Claudia Roquette-Pinto, Federico Barbosa and Antônio Moura.

In this anthology, there are poets from different parts of Brazil. They come not only from its main cultural centers, São Paulo (Arnaldo Antunes, Nelson Ascher, Lenora de Barros, Régis Bonvicino, Horácio Costa) and Rio de Janeiro (Carlito Azevedo, Ana Cristina Cesar, Angela de Campos, Claudia Roquette-Pinto), but also from Minas Gerais (Carlos Ávila, Júlio Castañon Guimarães, Francisco Alvim), the South of Brazil (Paulo Leminski, Josely Vianna Baptista), the North (Age de Carvalho), the Northeast (Waly Salomão, Duda Machado, Torquato Neto, and Federico Tavares Bastos Barbosa, who moved when very young to São Paulo), and from the Amazon forest (Antôntio Moura).

Paulo Leminski and Ana Cristina Cesar are leading figures. The humor and irreverence of Leminski's biting vocabulary and the subtle strangeness of Cesar's ambiguous "confessions" are, in fact, excellent examples of the varied and rich courses Brazilian poetry has taken in recent decades.

Besides being outstanding poets of their generation, Régis Bonvicino and Nelson Ascher have also written criticism and reviews and have been actively involved on editorial boards of poetry magazines and literary supplements. Both have also consistently translated poetry, including contemporary poetry from the United States. They are, therefore, excellent choices for this edition of the anthology.

I should add that this anthology has greatly benefited from having Michael Palmer, one of the highly distinguished American poets of his generation, as the advisor and editor for the translations. It has also counted upon the enthusiasm of poet Douglas Messerli, of Sun & Moon Press and Green Integer, who supervised the project.

—JOÃO ALMINO

INTRODUCTION

Modern poetry in Brazil is no less peculiar than the country itself. Brazil is a Latin American nation, but this does not tell the whole truth. It might be more accurate to say that Brazil is actually the other face of the South American subcontinent, not so much hidden as it is unknown. The same might be said of the country's literature in general and of poetry in particular.

The Iberian Baroque, Italian Arcadianism, French Romanticism, Parnassianism and Symbolism: all have held sway in Brazil at one time, each manifesting itself in a highly original way. Our history, however, begins around 1922, during the centennial celebrations of Brazil's independence from Portugal. That year, an eclectic group of young writers, poets, artists and musicians, most of them from São Paulo state's coffee-growing high bourgeoisie, came together to promote a Modern Art Week at the São Paulo Municipal Theater—a fairly faithful copy of the Paris Opera. French influence prevailed—Apollinaire and Cendrars along with Cubism, with a few touches of Italian Futurism.

The event left two important legacies: an ineradicable nonconformism in the face of provincial complacency, which took as its main aim to disprove any necessary link between social-political-economic underdevelopment and the status of the arts; and an increasingly fruitful relationship between the various branches of the arts. This contact was symbolically confirmed by the marriage of Oswald de Andrade, poet, writer, pamphleteer, playwright, critic and theoretician of Brazilian Modernism (not to be confused with the distinct movement of Hispanic Modernism) to the painter Tarsila do Amaral.

In the 1920s, Andrade wrote minimalist, anti-poetic poems and avant-garde novels, starting the Anthropophagic movement, whose aim was to swallow up foreign cultural influences and digest them Brazilian-style. He also wrote "Poesia Pau-Brasil" (Brazil-wood Poetry), a residual epic which, by mingling excerpts from historical chronicles and flashes of historical and geographical perception, redraws Brazilian history as an anti-epic, less by what is said than by what is insinuated between the lines. Andrade's concept of "anthropophagy" would be taken up in an original manner by the pop music of the 1960s. However, let us not get ahead of history.

The initial movement of Modernism in the 20s introduced into Brazilian poetry a global attitude, incorporating broad cultural interests, irreverence, humor, and free verse. In addition to Oswald de Andrade, some pioneers included Mário de Andrade, Raul Bopp and Luís Aranha. Modernism's great corpus, and arguably Brazilian poetry's finest hour, came in the 1930s, with the second wave of Modernists. The poetry of Carlos Drummond de Andrade, Murilo Mendes, Vinícius de Moraes and Manuel Bandeira, both individually and as a group, was equal to the principal currents of Western Modernism. The high quality of these poets is matched only by their sheer bad luck in having been confined to a readership, not only in their own tongue, but also in their own country, since they are exceedingly little known even in Portugal, a country whose poetic sensibility has taken paths substantially different from our own.

The poetry of the 1940s, today almost entirely forgotten, represents a reaction against Modernist principles. One poet originating from that decade, however, proved durable: João Cabral de Melo Neto. In addition to refining poetic techniques, he provided a synthesis of the novel's most representative trends and concerns. Using a poetic art mostly inherited from Drummond de Andrade, Cabral de Melo Neto incorporated traces of Northeastern themes common to many novelists of the period, particularly Graciliano Ramos. Of course, his poetry was not limited to these concerns, and Cabral de Melo Neto applied his method to a variety of issues, not least to a consideration of poetry itself.

During the following decade, Vinícius de Moraes, who had started his career as a poet nurturing rather vague metaphysical speculations interspersed with an interest in less universal, more concrete themes, began to mingle his interests with those of a new generation of popular music composers. Together they started a movement which would radically change the profile of pop music: the Bossa Nova. This movement, a confluence of Modernist diction with the urbanization and gentrification of rhythms, promoted a cooperation between so-called elite art *(pero no mucho)* and pop art *(ma non troppo)*. This cooperation would last for a good quarter of a century, reaching its peak in the musical movement of the 1960s, Tropicalism.

In a country where poetry is neither widely read nor taught, the status of Brazilian pop music is very sound, since every poet born since the 1950s not only stemmed from its roots but also, consciously or not, felt its influence. Any poet over the age of 45 who alleges otherwise is lying. That said, it should also be noted that, during this period, Brazilian pop music not only played a different role than pop music in the English speaking countries or in Hispanic America, but also constituted a substantial and diverse entity of its own whose more lasting influence would not be circumscribed by political or sentimental manifestations, but would seek through its lyrics a continuity with the tradition of poetry as such. More recently, Brazilian pop music has lost its creative drive, and no longer exercises a meaningful influence over poets.

The 1950s saw another movement which might be considered the third Modernist moment: Concretism. Led by Augusto de Campos, Haroldo de Campos and Décio Pignatari, its major drive may have been its placing of the intuitive program of 1922 on clearer grounds—hence the importance placed by Concretists on critical and theoretical debate; on filling in any of Modernism's lacunas, including the restoration of published works, not least those of Oswald de Andrade; and on updating and fine-tuning the continuing international effects of Modernism.

From the following decade on, Concrete poets trod more individual paths. Haroldo de Campos turned to a kind of prose poetry and to the so-called neo-Baroque. Décio Pignatari moved between Oswaldian prose and poetry, both visual and verse, while Augusto de Campos stayed fairthful to the movement's origins, developing and expanding its visual trends. Ferreira Gullar broke with these poets to launch neo-Concretism, later to embark on the project of poetry *engagé,* which he soon abandoned. Among the independent poets of the same generation (and therefore not included in this anthology), one might mention José Paulo Paes, Alfonso Avila and Sebastião Uchoa Leite. The latter, without affiliating himself with Concretism or later on, with Marginal poetry, left a significant body of poems. These poems, almost all of them metalinguistic in nature, combined the erudition of a Paul Valéry with comic strips and American B movies, shot through with a nihilist critique of reality, specifically Brazilian reality.

Modernist or Immaterial

This, then, is the background and environment against which the poets in this book began their work. It is worth noting at this point that the Concrete poets enriched the language with translations not only of modern poets (Pound, cummings, Mallarmé, Laforgue, Corbière and the Russians) but of earlier poetry (Provençal, *dolce stil nuovo*, the English Metaphysicals, and Chinese and Japanese classics). At least among poets, these influences ranked second only to those of Brazilian pop music. Through the work of these authors, the translation of poetry reached maturity and entered into a direct dialogue with living poets.

Contemporary Brazilian poetry stems from these precursors without being circumscribed by them. Apart from the distinct combination of influences that is inevitable for poets, individual personality and talent also play an integral part in their poetry.

Needless to say, during the three modernist "moments" we have mentioned, and even afterwards, much poetry was written which bore no resemblance to what we have just described. The issues were not an exclusive or exclusivist lineage, but simply whatever seems to have survived the test of time. Re-reading poets who did not join the mainstream is as melancholy as contemplating an outdated wardrobe. One example is much of the Marginal poetry of the 1970s, which whatever its limits, left us the still vital legacy of, among others, the work of Ana Cristina Cesar and of Francisco Alvim. Their trademark informality is not without consciousness of more craft-oriented poets such as Elizabeth Bishop, Murilo Mendes, and Manual Bandeira.

Indeed, one of the characteristics of Brazilian poetry of this century is the extent to which the success of individual talents has depended on their adhesion—dazzled or critical, playful or unwilling—to a minimal list of Modernist proposals. In fact, from 1922 on, Brazilian poetry has fallen into one of two categories: Modernist or immaterial. It is hard to say now whether this division was fate or more contingency: it is simply an empirical reality, verifiable by literary criticism's essentially rational criteria. This is an issue which neither theory nor the history of poetry has yet begun to examine.

For this reason, there is no common program for the poets of this book, no explicit consensus behind their writing. In fact, as opposed to the previous generation, these poets have shown little inclination toward the idea of belonging to a movement or school. Torquato Neto, for example, participated in Tropicalism, but soon afterwards abandoned it. In a very short span of time, Paulo Leminski moved from the geometric poem, which he was never to resume, to the exuberant prose of *Catatau*. The poets do have in common a set of concerns and poetic devices, however: there is the mainstream of an accepted tradition, as well as aims which, to a greater or lesser degree, all of them share.

Paradoxes

Paradoxically, poets from Brazilian Modernism on are unknown, owing less to their failure than to their success. Not only have they created many individual sets of poems (though that is surely true): they have created a literary universe of their own. Each one of them is, of course, connected with other universes, including those of French, German, Russian and Anglo-American poetry, but preferably acting through the whole.

There can be no *Weltliteratur* if the whole set of concerns and debates is not universalized. Thus, we are left in the odd position of having to define Brazilian poetry by what it is not.

From the 1960s on, Leminski, born in Southern Brazil in 1945, built a diverse work addressing issues both from the Modernism of the 1920s and Concretism of the 1950s. In that sense, Leminski has one exemplary poem. In the beginning, a seemingly banal statement: that every poet starting his career thinks he will be the greatest, but by the end comes to little. So far, so good. But the key to the poem is embedded in questions of address more subtle than those of *vousvoyer* and *tutoyer*. In the first, optimistic half of the poem, the subject is "a gente," a kind of colloquial "we," but meaning "I" which becomes, in the second, pessimistic part, a "we," indicated only by the verb, apparently the common first-person we, plural, but in fact the royal "we," symbol of the high rhetoric affected by the provincial elite. The poets Leminski invokes, as arguable as their sequence may be, only serve to illustrate the difference between the first "we" [a gente] and the second "we" [nós]. In short, the first is a kind of *yo el supremo* in the revolutionary state, whereas the second would be the same figure in exile, after the military coup.

In contrast with the exuberance of his prose and his personality, Leminski's poetry is notably concise. This concision is associated with voice and with the instaneous register of existence. This kind of concision, as seen in the Concrete poems of the 50s, had turned toward radical definitions of language, giving little place to a more explicit subjective register. Concision in the poetry of Leminski and Neto, as well as in the poetry of many poets anthologized here (Horácio Costa is one exception) emerges as both a linguistic fact and as the possibility for subjectivity. If Oswald de Andrade was the inventor of the so-called minute-poem, we might go so far as to say that Leminski has created the instant-poem, mingling Oswaldian concreteness with the anarchic-colloquial diction of pop singer Caetano Veloso and the Tropicalism of Torquato Neto. Concision. Exposing ideas in few words. Haiku. If in Leminski concision is conveyed as brevity, originating from the pressures of existence, in another poet of his generation, Duda Machado, concision is present as accuracy, as precision. Machado and

Leminski tread similar, but inverted, paths, the former departing from Tropicália and song lyrics towards a poetry of his own, completely different from that of Brazilian pop music. Leminski, on the other hand, a scholar after his fashion, continued to alternate between questions of high culture and nonsystematic incursions into the world of pop music. Concision. The coicidence of three early deaths: Neto, Ana Cristina Cesar and Leminski. Three suicides, the first two explicity, Leminski's implicit in his daily consumption of alcohol and drugs. Three journeys begun during or after the war, three poets who produced their main body of work during the military dictatorship, which ended only in 1985, when all three were dead or dying.

Concision within extension. After all, there are haikus where words abound, where three verses are three too many, as well as epic poems from which no word can be subtracted without harm. The poem between prose and poetry: this is the case of Josely Vianna Baptista, translator of Cuban novelist Lezama Lima's *Paradiso*, whose style could be considered a kind of brazilian neo-baroque: rhythms and images, fashioned by the "feeling for the measure," in the words of William Carlos Williams.

Horácio Costa seems to be an exception to this scenaario, following more openly the Hispanic discursive tradition, mediated through the American Beat generation. It is not surprising that Costa has lived in the United States and for several years in Mexico. Wally Salomão brings prose and poetry together, with satirical and metaphorical overtones.

Arnaldo Antunes operates in Neto's and Veloso's paradigm, highly privileging orality and visuality, as can be seen in his video-poem *Nome* (1944), which mingles pop music, electronic music, poetry and video. In this anthology, he presents texts which resume the instinctive-primitivist aspect of early Modernism.

Júlio Castañon Guimarães also writes concise poetry in the Minas Gerais style: lean, based on concrete facts and objects, often rough. This kind of roughness can be felt in the poetry of another poet from Minas Gerais, Carlos Ávila. Minas was the home state of Carlos Drummond de Andrade and Murilo Mendes: mountains, silence and iron ore. Age de Carvalho is the one, among all the poets here, who practices a poetry of a more abstract nature. People and places are referred to fragmentarily; his imagination is often quite rhetorical, although his writings are short and sharp. Lenora de Barros' work covers urban themes, emphasizing the existing tensions of a large city like São Paulo, where she lives. While Barros' is a work close to plastic art, the poetry of Claudia Roquette-Pinto and Angela de Campos, both Rio de Janeiro-based poets, in contrast, engages feminist themes maintaining a different, introspective dialogue with visuality. Carlos Azevedo, although a beginner, merits already some attention. There are two very new voices in this book: Federico Tavares Bastos Barbosa and Antônio Moura. The general criterion for poem selection was how clearly the poet's procedures were conveyed.

It is well worth mentioning that nearly all the poet's in this selection worked as publishers or collaborators for alternative journals in the 1970s and 1980s, such as *Navilouca* (Torquato Neto), *Pólen* (Duda Machado), *Qorpo Estranho, 1* (Carlos Ávila), and *Almanak 80* (Arnaldo Antunes). These journals, along with *Código*, published in Bahia, acted as a laboratory where the impacts of Concrete poetry and Tropicalism were re-examined. At the same time, these publications served as a shelter for work with no prospect for commerical publication at the time. Another feature common to most of the poets in this book: they are translators. Leminski translated, among others, Samuel Beckett and Lawrence Ferlinghetti; Castañon translated Francis Ponge and Michel Butor; Duda Machado, Gustave Flaubert, etc. These translations speak to a need to enrich a poetry which, strangely enough, has nothing in common with the poetry from Portugal or Hispanic America. The latter, discursive and deeply marked by Surrealism, never quite established its grip on Brazilian writers.

Once again, the late Elizabeth Bishop must be mentioned. She organized one of two Brazilian poetry anthologies for the Anglo-American world: *An Anthology of Twentieth-Century Brazilian Poetry* with Emanuel Brasil, published in 1972 by Wesleyan University Press. That book included Oswald de Andrade, Manuel Bandeira, Mário de Andrade, Carlos Drummond de Andrade, Murilo Mendes, Cecília Meireles, Jorge de Lima, João Cabral de Melo Neto, Vinícius de Moraes and Ferreira Gullar. Soon afterward, Emanuel Brasil oversaw the publishing of *Brazilian Poetry: 1950-1980,* also published by Wesleyan, representing poets linked to Concretism, as well as some independent writers.

Anthologies always run the risk of excessive partiality or superficiality. We hope to have kept these evils at a distance. However, it should be clear that other selections can and must be made. Among the younger poets, there are many promising names not included in this book, among them Beatriz Azevedo, Heitor Ferraz, Guilherme Mansur, and Mércia Pessoa. This book is only our current reading of what is most significant and representative in modern Brazilian poetry. Nothing the sun could not explain!

—RÉGIS BONVICINO AND NELSON ASCHER

Translated by Regina Alfarano and Dana Stevens

Francisco Alvim
1938

Born in Araxá, Minas Gerais state, in 1938, Francisco Alvim grew up in the area between Rio de Janeiro and Belo Horizonte. Upon the publication of his first book, *Sol dos cegos* (1968), he traveled to Paris, where he lived from 1969 to 1971. After returning to Brazil he published *Passatempo* (Pass Time) in 1974 in the pioneering marginal collection "Frenesi." In 1981, Brasilense Publishing House collected nearly all his work in one volume, *Poesias Reunidas* (1968-1988). Another book, *Claro Enigma* was also published in 1988 and his *O Elefante* in 2000. For several years Alvim served as a diplomat in Spain before retiring to Rio de Janeiro, where he now lives.

ADOLFO MONTEJO NAVAS

BOOKS OF POETRY:

Sol dos cegos (Rio de Janeiro: Edição do autor, 1968); *Passatempo* (Rio de Janeiro: Caleção Frenesi, 1974); *Exemplar Proceder* (Rio de Janeiro: Edição, 1975); *Lago, Montanha* (Rio de Janeiro: Coleção Capricho, 1981); *Poesias Reunidas* (1968-1988); *Claro Enigma* (1988); *O Elefante* (São Paulo: Cia das Letras, 2000)

A Pedra

Árvores me atropelam
folhas e galhos dentro de mim,
vazio de tudo o que sou
verifico que os vegetais, como as pedras,
apodrecem

(from *Sol dos cegos,* 1968)

Um corredor

um corredor enorme
estes que vejo todos caminhando
que todos me vêem caminhando

um enorme corredor enorme
este que tanta gente caminha
eu todos caminham

um corredor que caminha
eu todos a gente
um corredor se caminha

(from *Passatempo,* 1974)

The Stone

Trees crush me
leaves and branches inside me,
void of all that I am
I can confirm that plants, like stones,
go rotten

—Translated from the Portuguese by Dana Stevens

A Corridor

An enormous corridor
that I see everybody walking
that everybody sees me walking

An enormous enormous corridor (enormous)
that so many of us walk
I everybody walks

A corridor that walks
I everybody us
A corridor walks (itself)

—Translated from the Portuguese by Thomas Colchie and the author

Luz

Em cima da cômoda
uma lata, dois jarros, alguns objetos
entre eles três antigas estampas
Na mesa duas toalhas dobradas
uma verde, outra azul
um lençol também dobrado livros chaveiro
Sob o braço esquerdo
um caderno de capa preta
em frente uma cama
cuja cabeceira abriu-se numa grande fenda
Na parede alguns quadros

Um relógio, um copo

(from *Passatempo*, 1974)

Revolução

Antes da revolução eu era professor
Com ela veio a demissão da Universidade
Passei a cobrar posições, de mim e dos outros
(meus pais eram marxistas)
Melhorei nisso—
hoje já não me maltrato
nem a ninguém

(from *Exemplar Proceder*, 1975)

Light

On top of the dresser
a can, two jars, some things
among them three old prints
On the table, two folded tablecloths
one green, the other blue
a sheet, also folded, books, a keychain
Under my right arm
a black-covered notebook
In front, a bed
whose headboard has cracked wide open
On the wall some paintings

A clock, a cup

—Translated from the Portuguese by Dana Stevens

Revolution

Before the revolution I was a professor
With it came my dismissal from the University
I began to demand positions, from myself and others
(my parents were Marxists)
I've grown better in this—
today I no longer mistreat myself
or anyone else

—Translated from the Portuguese by Dana Stevens

Leopoldo

Minha namorada cocainômana
me procura nas madrugadas
para dizer que me ama
Fico olhando as olheiras dela
(tão escuras quanto a noite lá fora)
onde escondo minha paixão
Quando nos amamos
peço que me bata
me maltrate fundo
pois amo demais meu amor
e as manhãs empalidecem rápido

(from *Lago, Montanha*, 1981)

Frases Feitas

aí ele disse:
Não sou rico mas tenho alguns cristais
Viu que eu continuava sério
A gente não deve se sujar
por pouca coisa

(from *Lago, Montanha*, 1981)

Flor Da Idade

A tarde parou na janela
úmida verde
ela acabou de sair
nos despedimos sem tristeza

(from *Lago, Montanha*, 1981)

Leopold

My coked-up girlfriend
seeks me out at dawn
to tell me she loves me
I look at the shadows under her eyes
(as dark as the night outside)
where my passion hides
When we make love
I ask her to beat me
mistreat me deeply
for I love my love so much
and morning pales so rapidly

—Translated from the Portuguese by Dana Stevens

Set Phrases

so then he said:
I'm not rich but I've got some crystal
He saw I wasn't laughing
Why sully ourselves
for so little

—Translated from the Portuguese by Dana Stevens

The Bloom of Youth

Afternoon stopped in the window
green and wet
she just walked out
we parted without regret

—Translated from the Portuguese by Dana Stevens

Arnaldo Antunes
1960

Born in São Paulo in 1960, Arnaldo Antunes attended the University of São Paulo, but did not complete his degree. He edited several poetry magazines: *Almanak 80* (1980), *Kataloki* (1981), and *Atlas* (1988). Among his published books are *Ou E*, a book of visual poems (1983), *Psia* (1986), *Tudos* (1990) and *As Coisas* (1992). Almost all of his books have gone through several editions.

VLADIMIR FONTES

Also a musician and visual artist, Antunes participated in several exhibitions of visual poetry both in Brazil and abroad during the period from 1983 to 1994. He put together the rock group Titãs with which he released several albums between 1982 and 1992. In 1993, *Nome* (in video, book form, and CD) was released. This work is a multimedia project including poetry, music and computer animation in partnership with Celia Catunda, Kiko Mistrorigo and Zaba Moreau. It was exhibited at shows and festivals worldwide and received honors at the First Annual New York Video Festival. As a musician, Antunes has released a number of recordings in recent years. In 1999 he wrote a sound track for the dance company O Corpo. And in 2000, Antunes published a book about pop music and poetry titled *Quarenta Escritos* (São Paulo: Iluminuras).

BOOKS OF POETRY:

Ou E (1986); *Psia* (São Paulo: Iluminuras Projetos e Produçõs Editoriais, 1986); *Tudos* (São Paulo: Iluminuras Projetos e Produçõs Editoriais, 1990); *As Coisas* (São Paulo: Iluminuras Projetos e Produçõs Editoriais, 1992); *Nome* (with Celia Catunda, Kiko Mistrorigo, and Zaba Moreau) (São Paulo: BMG Ariola Discos, 1993); *ONLY 2 ou mais corpos no mesmo espaço* (São Paulo: Editorial Perspectiva, 1997)

ENGLISH LANGUAGE TRANSLATIONS:

Nome [no translator listed] (São Paulo: Arnaldo Antunes and Zaba Moreau, 1993).

poema musicado

(from *Psia*, 1986)

As pedras são muito mais lentas do que os animais. As plantas exalam mais cheiro quando a chuva cai. As andorinhas quando chega o inverno voam até o verão. Os pombos gostam de milho e de migalhas de pão. As chuvas vêm da água que o sol evapora. Os homens quando vêm de longe trazem malas. Os peixes quando nadam juntos formam um cardume. As larvas viram borboletas dentro dos casulos . Os dedos dos pés evitam que se caia. Os sábios ficam em silêncio quando os outros falam. As máquinas de fazer nada não estão quebradas. Os rabos dos macacos servem como braços. Os rabos dos cachorros servem como risos. As vacas comem duas vezes a mesma comida. As páginas foram escritas para serem lidas. As árvores podem viver mais tempo que as pessoas. Os elefantes e golfinhos têm boa memória. Palavras podem ser usadas de muitas maneiras. Os fósforos só podem ser usados uma vez. Os vidros quando estão bem limpos quase não se vê. Chicletes são pra mastigar mas não para engolir. Os dromedários têm uma corcova e os camelos têm duas. As meia-noites duram menos do que os meio-dias. As tartarugas nascem em ovos mas não são aves. As baleias vivem na água mas não são peixes. Os dentes quando a gente escova ficam brancos. Cabelos quando ficam velhos ficam brancos. As músicas dos índios fazem cair chuva. Os corpos dos mortos enterrados adubam a terra. Os carros fazem muitas curvas pra subir a serra. Crianças gostam de fazer perguntas sobre tudo. Nem todas as respostas cabem num adulto.

(from *Tudos*, 1992)

poem set to music

—*Translated from the Portuguese by Dana Stevens*

Stones are much slower than animals. Plants give off more scent when it rains. Swallows fly south for the winter. Doves like corn and breadcrumbs. Rain comes from water that the sun evaporates. When men come from far off, they bring suitcases. Fish swimming together form a school. Caterpillars become butterflies in their cocoons. Toes keep you from falling. Wise men are quiet when others speak. Machines for doing nothing are not broken. Monkeys' tails are used as arms. Dogs' tails are used as smiles. Cows eat the same food twice. Pages are written to be read. Trees live longer than people. Elephants and dolphins have good memories. Words can be used in many ways. Matches can only be used once. When glass is clean you can hardly see it. Gum is to chew but not to swallow. Dromedaries have one hump and camels have two. Midnights are shorter than middays. Turtles hatch from eggs but aren't birds. Whales live in water but aren't fish. Teeth turn white when you brush them. Hair turns white when it gets old. The songs of Indians make rain fall. Buried bodies of the dead fertilize the earth. Cars make many curves to climb a mountain. Children like to ask questions about everything. Not all the answers fit in an adult.

—*Translated from the Portuguese by Regina Alfarano and Dana Stevens*

As   coisas   têm   peso,
massa,   volume,   tamanho,
tempo,   forma,   cor,   posição,
textura,   duração,
densidade,   cheiro,
valor,consistência,   pro-
fundidade,   contorno,
temperatura,   função,
aparência,   preço,   destino,
idade,   sentido.   As   coisas
não têm paz.

(from *As Coisas*, 1992)

algo é o nome do homem
coisa é o nome do homem
homem é o nome do cara
isso é o nome da coisa
cara é o nome do rosto
fome é o nome do moço
homem é o nome do troço
osso é o nome do fóssil
corpo é o nome do morto
homem é o nome do outro

(from *Nome*, 1993)

Quase

agagueiraquasepalavra
quaseaborta
apalavraquasesilêncio
quasetransborda
osilêncioquaseeco

(previously unpublished)

T h i n g s   h a v e   w e i g h t ,
m a s s ,   v o l u m e ,   s i z e ,
t i m e ,   f o r m ,   c o l o r ,
p o s i t i o n ,   t e x t u r e ,   d u r a -
t i o n ,   d e n s i t y ,   s m e l l ,
w o r t h ,   c o n s i s t e n c y ,
d e p t h ,   c o n t o u r ,   t e m p e r -
a t u r e ,   f u n c t i o n ,   a p p e a r -
a n c e ,   p r i c e ,   d e s t i n y ,   a g e ,
m e a n i n g .   T h i n g s   h a v e   n o
p e a c e .

—*Translated from the Portuguese by Regina Alfarano and Dana Stevens*

something is the man's name
thing is the man's name
man is the guy's name
this is the thing's name
face is the head's name
hunger is the boy's name
man is the stuff's name
bone is the fossil's name
body is the dead's name
man is the other's name

—*Translated from the Portuguese by Dana Stevens*

Almost

thestammeralmostword
almostaborts
thewordalmostsilence
almostoverflows
thesilencealmostecho

—*Translated from the Portuguese by Regina Alfarano and Dana Stevens*
Previously unpublished

Nelson Ascher
1958

FOTO: CLAUDIA GUIMARÃES

Born in São Paulo in 1958, Nelson Ascher majored in Business Administration at Fundação Getúlio Vargas, but never worked in that field. A literary critic for *Folha de S. Paulo* since 1984, he was the founder and editor of *Revista da USP* from 1988 to 1994. His books of poetry include *Ponta da Lingua* (1983) and *Sonho da Razão* (1993). His most recent book of poetry is *Algo de Sol* (1996).

Ascher is perhaps best known as a translator. His translations include *Vida sem fim* (in collaboration with Paulo Leminski) by Lawrence Ferlinghetti, *Folhetim: poemas traduzidos* (1987), *Canção antes da ceifa—posia húngara moderna* (1990), and *Quase uma elegia* (1995), a selection of Joseph Brodsky's poetry. He has also published a volume of political and polemical essays mainly about Central and Eastern Europe, dealing with the fall of communism, the Yugoslav civil war, German reunification and the Holocaust: *Pomos da Discórdia* (1966). His most recent collection of translations is *Poesia Alheia*, published by Imago press in 1998.

BOOKS OF POETRY:

Ponta da Lingua (São Paulo: privately published: 1983); *O Sonho da Razão* [published with *Ponta da Lingua*] (Rio de Janeiro: Editora 34, 1993); *Algo de Sol* (Rio de Janeiro: Editora 34, 1996).

Meu Coraçao

Mein Herz, mein Herz ist träurig
HEINE

Se tenho um coração maior que
o mundo, por que seus ventrículos
fecham-se em pontos tão ridículos
quando oxigênio algum retorque

as carências da carne? à parte
isso, o lipídio sujo encarde o
sangue que irriga o miocárdio
por dentro até que o seu enfarte

maciço torne enfim as várias
figuras líricas, diletas—
letais. Dizei-me, enfim, poetas:
o amor entope as coronárias?

(from *Ponta da Lingua*, 1983)

Onde Há Fumaça

dann steigt ihr als Rauch in die Luft
PAUL CELAN

Fumaça alguma implica
memória, já que as coisas
se perdem na fumaça
que, assim, tampouco pode

tornar-se um monumento,
pois sendo transitória
nem mesmo homenageia
a transitoriedade.

Fumaça enquanto tinta,
embora branca (um branco
mais palidez de horror
qua alvura de inocência),

My Heart

Mein Herz, mein Herz ist träurig
                        HEINE

If my heart is larger than
the world, why then do these ventricles
close down into ridiculous points
when no oxygen at all replies

to the needs of the flesh? What's more,
the dense lipid stains
the blood that floods the myocardium
internally until a massive

stroke finally turns the various
lyric figures, so esteemed—
lethal. Then, poets, do tell me:
can love clog the coronaries?

—Translated from the Portuguese by Regina Alfarano

Where There's Smoke

dann steigt ihr als Rauch in die Luft
                        PAUL CELAN

No smoke implies
memory, since things
are lost in smoke
which cannot thus

become a monument,
for being transitory, it
pays no homage
even to transitoriness.

Smoke as ink,
though white (a white more
of horror's pallor
than purity's innocence),

serve talvez à escrita;
porém, não há destreza
que inscreva na fumaça,
como na pedra, um nome.

Quando a fumaça, quase
vegetativa, irrompe e,
traindo o genealógico,
assume aspecto arbóreo,

não cabe preguntar
acerca (onde há fumaçca,
há cinzas) das raízes
mais fundas da fumaça.

(from *O Sonho da Razão,* 1993)

Amor

O olhar desapropria
a forma alheia, o ouvido
sequestra a voz alheia,
o olfato rapta o odor

alheio, o paladar
rouba o sabor alheio,
o tato furta a carne
alheia, ou seja, a própria;

reluz o olhar alheio
do visto em outro, ecoa
o ouvido alheio um outro,
rescende o olfato alheio

a um outro, sabe a um outro
o paladar alheio,
tateia o tato alheio
um outro, ou seja, o mesmo.

(from *O Sonho da Razão,* 1993)

may serve for writing;
but where's the skill
that inscribes a name,
in smoke, as in a rock?

When smoke, near-
vegetal, erupts and,
betraying genealogy,
takes on arboreal shape,

one mustn't ask
about (where there's smoke,
there's ash) the deepest
roots of smoke.

—Translated from the Portuguese by Dana Stevens

Love

Sight dispossesses
the form of the other, hearing
sequesters the voice of the other,
smell abducts the odor

of the other, taste
steals the flavor of the other,
touch snatches the flesh
of the other, that is, one's own;

the look of the other gleams
from what is seen in another,
the ear of the other echoes another,
the scent of the other rises

to another, the flavor of the other
tastes of another
the other touch palpates another
that is, the very same.

—Translated from the Portuguese by Regina Alfarano

Bashô em Paris

para Rose

Manhã de gala:
flores, imóveis
damas desnudas,
desfilam cores.

Midi le juste:
suicida, o sol,
no mar de suor,
se põe a pino.

Tarde-alfarrábio:
folhas em verde,
como as impressas,
amarelescem.

Que noite albina!
A torre, embora
de ferro, quase
treme de frio.

(from *O Sonho da Razão*, 1993)

Máquinas

Se—máquinas precisas
que somos de morrer—
nossa função implica
memória ininterrupta,

por que, afinal, possuis
(lubrificadamente
contrátil entre as pernas)
o teu lagar de amnésia?

(from *Algo de Sol*, 1996)

Basho In Paris

for Rose

Gala morning:
flowers, motionless
naked ladies,
parade colors.

Midi le juste:
suicidal, the sun,
in a sea of sweat,
sets at high noon.

Second-hand afternoon:
leaves of green,
like printed sheets,
turn yellow.

Albino night!
The tower, though
iron, almost
shivers from cold.

—*Translated from the Portuguese by Regina Alfarano*

Machines

If—precise machines
for dying that we are—
our function implies
unending memory,

why, then, do you bear
(lubriciously
contractile between your legs)
your wine-press of amnesia?

—*Translated from the Portuguese by Regina Alfarano*

Flagrante

Opaco, mas translúcido
durante o ocaso, como
pomar onde a ramagem
das árvores frutíferas

admite obliquamente
a luz emaranhada,
o *nylon* do vestido
que vestes filtra o sol

exangue, cujos raios,
a fim de desenhar-te,
imbricam-se num último
flagrante, que dirime

a sede da retina
na qual se imprime (nítida
radiografia) o teu
contorno curvilíneo.

(from *Algo de Sol,* 1996)

Snapshot

Opaque, but translucent
at sunset, like
an orchard where branches
of bearing trees

obliquely admit
the tangled light,
the nylon of the dress
you wear filters the

bloodless sun, whose rays,
in their attempt to draw you,
betray themselves in a final
snapshot appeasing

the retina's thirst
to imprint there (vivid
x-ray) your
curving shape.

—Translated from the Portuguese by Regina Alfarano

Carlos Ávila
1955

Born in Belo Horizonte, Minas Gerais, in 1955, Carlos Ávila is a poet and journalist. He edited and participated in several avant-garde journals. He is the son of the noted Brazilian poets Afonso Ávila and Laís Correa do Araujo, both linked to the concretism movement. His poetry publications include the books *Acqui & Agora* (1981) and *Sinal de Menos* (1989), and published *Asperos* (1990) and *Bissexto Sentido* of 1999. He continues also to publish essays in journals and newspapers in Brazil and abroad. From 1995-1999 Ávila edited the Suplemmento Literário de Minas Gerais, a monthly newspaper of poetry.

BOOKS OF POETRY:

Acqui & Agora (1981); *Sinal de Menos* (1989); *Asperos* (1990); *Bissexto Sentido* (São Paulo: Editora perspectiva, 1999)

Baudelaire Sob O Sol

O sol
(a ser adjetivado:
im-pla-cá-vel)
descourou a capa
de um volume de baudelaire

as flores do mal
(descubro)
não resistem à lenta
violência do sol
(sol de boca-de-sertão
que estorrica o solo?)

também
quem mandou
colocar a estante
nesta posição:
o que estaria baudelaire
(em efigie gráfica)
fazendo no sertão?

se as flores do mal
não suportam o sol
(résponde baudelaire)
reistiriam aos punhais
do óxido e do sal?

(previously unpublished)

Baudelaire Answer

The sun
(awaiting an adjective:
im-pla-ca-ble)
bleached the cover
of a volume of baudelaire

the flowers of evil
(I discover)
cannot resist the sun's
slow violence
(sun of the backlands' mouth
that blasts the land dry?)

besides,
who had
the shelf
put there:
what would baudelaire
(in graphic effigy)
be doing in the backlands?

if the flowers of evil
can't stand the sun
(answers baudelaire)
how could they resist the thrusts
of salt and rust?

—*Translated from the Portuguese by Regina Alfarano*

Narcissus Poeticus

secou

(no vaso
 sem água)

mal plantado
numa waste land
(minúscula)
de apartamento sombrio:
como resistir
a pó poeira poluição?

maltratado ex-narciso
à própria sorte abandonado
(rente ao piso)
sem fonte
nem espelho

secou
(só no vaso)
sem suor nem saliva
sem lágrima
que o pudesse salvar

morreu
(fuligem
na alma)

(previously unpublished)

Narcissus Poeticus

dried up

(in a waterless
vase)

ill planted
in a (tiny)
waste land
of the dim apartment:
how to resist
dust dirt pollution?

mistreated ex-narcissus
abandoned to its fate
(flat on the floor)
without well
or mirror

dried up
(alone in the vase)
without sweat or saliva
or tears
to save it

died
(soot
on its soul)

—*Translated from the Portuguese by Regina Alfarano*

Carlito Azevedo
1961

Azevedo was born in Rio de Janeiro in 1961. He has published several books of poetry, including *Collapus Linguae* (1991), which received the Juabti Poetry Prize, *As Banhistas* (1993) and *Sob a noite física* (1996). His translations of poetry and prose include Max Jacob, René Char, and Jean Follain. He is currently the director of the Circle of Poetic Research in Rio de Janeiro, and he earns his living from his poetry. He is currently the editor of the Rio de Janeiro based *Inimigo Rumor*, one of the most noted of Brazilian poetry magazines.

VLADIMIR FONTES

BOOKS OF POETRY:

Collapus Linguae (São Paulo: Imago, 1991); *As Banhistas* (São Paulo: Imago, 1993); *Sob a noite físcia* (Rio de Janeiro: Editora Sette Letras, 1996);

ENGLISH LANGUAGE TRANSLATIONS:

poems in "Lies About the Truth: An Anthology of Brazilian Poetry," edited by Régis Bonvicino in collaboration with Tarso M. de Melo, in *New American Writing*, no. 18 (2000).

Na Noite Gris

Na noite gris
este fulgor
no ar? Tigres

à espreita? Claro
sol de um cigarro
em lábios-lis?

Na lixa abrupta
súbita chispa?
Choque de peles

a contra-pelo
(tal numa rua
escura mutua-

mente se enlaçam
as contra-luzes
de dois faróis)?

(from *Collapus Linguae*, 1991)

In Grey Night

In grey night
this luster
in air? Tigers

lurking? Pale
sun of a cigarette
at lily-lips?

In sandpaper's roughness
a sudden glare?
The shock of skins

against hair
(as in a dark
street doub-

ly enlace
the counterbeams
of two headlights)?

—*Translated from the Portuguese by Dana Stevens*

Fábula (Real) dos Lagos do México

Para Enylton de Sá Rego e Sarah

Veja estes
lagos de montanha

irão secar

(como da fruta o
azedo do carvão o êxodo da
cor como fibrilas cristais vítreos
xistosidades como tudo o
que a vista vê)

mas deles

mas da larva dispensando
brânquias e
nadadeiras

despertará adulta
agora já a

salamandra

ex-larva
axolotl tigrinum

que nenhum sol
há de secar

(from *Collapus Linguae*, 1991)

(Real) Fable of the Lakes of Mexico

For Enylton de Sá Rego and Sarah

Look at those
mountain lakes

they will dry up

(as of the fruit the
sour from the coal the exodus from the
color like fibrils crystals vitreous
foliations like all that
which the sight sees)

but from them

but from the larva dispensing
branchias and
flippers

will awaken adult
now the

salamander

ex-larva
axolotl tigrinum

that no sun
will dry up

*—Translated from the Portuguese by Marta Bentley and
Scott Bentley*

Banhista

Apenas
     em frente
ao mar
         um dia de verão—
quando tua voz
            acesa percorresse,
consumindo-o,
          o pavio de um verso
até sua última
           sílaba inflamável—
quando o súbito
          atrito de um nome
em tua memória te
         incendiasse os cabelos—
(e sobre tua pele
        de fogo a
brisa fizesse
     rasgaduras
de água)

(from *As Banhistas,* 1993)

Bather

Barely
    before
the sea
    one summer's day—
when your voice,
    lit, traversed,
consuming it,
    the wick of a poem
until its last
    tindered syllable—
when the sudden
    friction of a name
in your memory
    set your hair ablaze—
(and on your skin
    of fire a
breeze ripped
    like water)

—Translated from the Portuguese by Dana Stevens

Ouro Preto

Anjo não, *Anjo*:
como se um sopro
lhe sobre as asas
batesse e quase

voasse e caso
voasse sendo
leveza menos
que exatidão.

Anjo de igreja
ao ar aberto
(a nave: a nuvem?)

sabeis a pedra-
sabão, melhor,
a bolha-de-.

(from *As Banhistas,* 1993)

A Margarida-Pérola

Severo e estranho rumo
conduz-nos ao mais puro
prazer: roçar a pétala
da margarida-pérola,
luzente, eletrizando-se
no atrito entanto doce;
fazer vergar num átimo
de tempo, ao fogo, o sândalo
que a nada então reduz-se,
silente, à ação da luz e
calor. Exala o cheiro-
madeleine de um chiqueiro,
no pratos o porco, istmo
de podre e preciosismo.

(from *Sob a noite física,* 1996)

Ouro Preto

Not an angel, an *Angel*:
as if a breeze
beat over his wings
and nearly

flew and if it
flew was less
lightness
than precision.

Church angel
in open air
(boat: cloud?)

you taste of soap-
stone, the best,
the bubble of.

—Translated from the Portuguese by Dana Stevens

Pearl-Daisy

Severe and strange course
leads us to the purest
pleasure: to graze the petal
of the pearl-daisy
shining, self-electrifying
in the gentle friction;
to make it bend in
a nanosecond, the sandalwood then,
in the fire, shrinks to nothing,
silent under the force of heat
and light. It exhales the *madeleine-*
scent of a pigsty,
pig on the plate, strait
of preciosity and rot.

—Translated from the Portuguese by Michael Palmer

Relendo Saxífraga

A flor de luz febril
do gozo medra em misto
de covardia e brio.

Mas mina o corpo (a rocha
do corpo) e logo em fúria
e em fogo desabrocha.

Quer ir além do corpo?
por onde aéreas pétalas
de nada ou de torpor?

O olhar pára, decifra
(garança entre vermelhos)
um perfume em *Saxífraga.*

(from *Sob a noite física,* 1996)

Rereading Saxifrage

The febrile light-flower
of desire swells into a mix
of courage and cowardice.

But it undermines the body (the rock
of the body) and soon it blooms
in fury and fire.

Wants to transcend the body?
toward aerial petals
of stupor and emptiness?

The gaze halts, deciphers
(rose-madder among reds)
a scent in *Saxifrage*.

—Translated from the Portuguese by Michael Palmer

Mulher

Rude calcário
lacera a pele
fina, de arroz;

carícia oculta
corais, e luvas
mudam-se em puas;

cristal, graveto,
farpa, granito:
qualquer palavra

fere este corpo
(que entanto a guarda
e afia como

novo esqueleto:
interno em gume,
externo em grito).

(from *Sob a noite física,* 1996)

Woman

Rough calcareous
lacerates the fine
skin, of rice;

occult caress
corals, and gloves
change themselves into prongs;

crystal, kindling,
splinter, granite:
any word

wounds this body
(that meanwhile guards
and sharpens as

a new skeleton:
internal in edge,
external in scream).

*—Translated from the Portuguese by Marta Bentley and
Scott Bentley*

Lenora de Barros
1953

Lenora de Barros was born on November 6, 1953 in São Paulo. Since 1975, Barros has contributed visual poetry both to Brazilian and international publications such as *Qorpo, Estranho, Flue,* and *Poliester.* Her first book was *Onde se vê* (1983). In 1984 she participated in the XVIIth Bienal de Sáo Paulo with videotext visual poems. She also has shown in the Muestra Internacional de Libros de Artista in Argentina. Individual exhibits followed in Italy, which represented work from 1975 to 1990. Barros has also curated many exhibits, both at home and abroad. She contributed CD-ROM interactive poems to the *Arte Cidadae* in São Paulo. She has translated Octavio Paz (*El Mono Gramático*) and is currently preparing a book, *Nada haver.*

In recent years she has become a visual artist, showing her work in the important space, Galeria Millan in São Paulo.

BOOKS OF POETRY:

Onde se vê (1983)

A Cidade Ácida

a cidade
ácida
asfixia

oxida
a palavra
poesia

o poema vem
de outros ares
de outros óxidos
e oxigênios

infiltra a seco
a umidade fria

o

pingue
pongue
oculto

que ali mina
gota a gota

o som sopro
do sentido
vida

(previously unpublished)

Acid City

the a-
cid city
asphyxiates

oxidizes
the word
poetry

the poem comes
from other airs
from other oxides
and oxygens

dry infiltration
of cold humidity

the

secret
ping
pong

undermining
drop by drop

the soughing sound
of sense
life

—*Translated from the Portuguese by Michael Palmer*

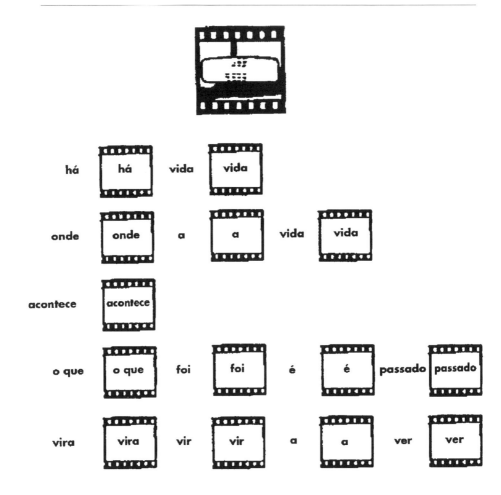

(previously unpublished)

THERE IS THERE IS LIFE LIFE

WHERE WHERE THE THE LIFE LIFE

HAPPENS HAPPENS

WHAT WHAT WAS WAS IS IS PAST PAST

TURNS TURNS WILL COME WILL COME TO TO SEE SEE

—*Translated from the Portuguese by Michael Palmer*

Régis Bonvicino
1955

Bonvicino was born in São Paulo, where he has re-
mained to become a central figure in Brazilian po-
etics. He graduated from law school in 1978, and
works as a judge. But his major energies are devoted
to poetry, as a translator—of Oliverio Girondo, Jules
Laforge, and several American poets including
Michael Palmer, Douglas Messerli, and Robert
Creeley—as an editor and poet.

   In the 1970s and 1980s Bonvicino edited several
poetry journals, in particular *Poesia em Greve* (1975),
Qorpo Estranho (1976-1982), and *Muda* (1977). He
is currently the editor of Brazilian poetry for *Serta*, a
journal published in Madrid, Spain. He also writes
criticism and has reviewed numerous books for the major São Paulo newspaper, *Folha de S.
Paulo*.

   Among his poetry books are *Ossos de Barboleta, 33 Poems, Más companhias, Primeiro Tempo*,
and a children's book, *num zoológico de letras*. His poetry is filled with the imagery of nature,
with the flora and fauna of Brazil; but it is also a poetry very much about the urban landscape of
São Paulo where he lives. And while his poems often contain narrative passages, for the most
part Bonvicino's work is centered on the play of sound and syntax, of rhyme and intense rhyth-
mic shifts. His work is at once playful and wise, a poetry recognizing the serendipity of our lives
while lyrically pointing to beauty everywhere around us, even it if is often covered over with
urban blight.

   Most recently, Bonvicino collaborated with four American poets, Charles Bernstein, Dou-
glas Messerli, Norma Cole and Guy Bennett, in *Duetos*. After co-editing the anthology, *Nothing
the Sun Could Not Explain: 20 Contemporary Brazilian Poets* in 1997 (upon which this anthol-
ogy is based), he edited a selection of Brazilian poetry in *New American Writing* (2000). He is
currently working on new translations of work by Michael Palmer and Charles Bernstein. In
2000 Green Integer published a translation in English of his poetry, *Sky-Eclipse: Selected Poems*.
He is currently writing for *O Estado de S. Pāulo*, one of the major Brazilian newspapers.

BOOKS OF POETRY:

Bicho Papel (São Paulo: Edições Greve, 1975); *Régis Hotel* (São Paulo: Edições Greve, 1978);
Sósia da Cópia; Más Companhias (São Paulo: Editora Olavobrás, 1987); *33 Poemas* (São Paulo:
Editora Illminuras, 1990); *Outros Poemas* (São Paulo: Editora Iluminuras, 1993); *Primeiro Tempo*
[collecting *Sósia da Cópia, Régis Hotel* and *Bicho Papel*] (São Paulo: Editora Perspectiva, 1995),
Ossos de Borboleta (São Paulo: Editora 34, 1996); *Céu-eclipse* (São Paulo: Editora 34, 1999); *Me
transformo ou O Filho de Sêmele* (São Paulo: Tigre do espelho, 1999); *Lindero Nuevo Vedado:*

Antologia Poetica (Lisbon: Édições Quasi, 2002)

ENGLISH LANGUAGE TRANSLATIONS:

Sky-Eclipse: Selected Poems, trans. by numerous translators (København and Los Angeles: Green Integer, 2000); selected poems in "Lies About the Truth: An Anthology of Brazilian Poetry," edited by Régis Bonvicino in collaboration with Tarso M. de Melo, in *New American Writing*, no. 18 (2000)

Não Nada

Não nada ainda do outro
semelhante ainda ao mesmo
mínimo ainda o outro
ele mesmo não ainda outro
de um mesmo morto outro
insulado em seu corpo

Vincos do mesmo ainda
no íntimo do outro tampouco
cicatrizes unem
tatuagens dissipam
antenas clavadas, em tinta
cacos do outro estilhaços do outro

Uma borboleta fixa encobre
cicatrizes num corpo

(from *Outros Poemas*, 1993)

No Nothing

No nothing still the other
similar still to the same
minimal still the other
he himself not yet the other
of the same dead another
secluded in his body

Traces still of the same
deep inside the other not yet
scars link
tattoos dissipate
bludgeoned antennas, in ink
shards of the other splinters of the other

A stilled butterfly screens
scars on a body

*—Translated from the Portuguese by Regina Alfarano,
revised by Dana Stevens*

A Desordem De

A desordem de sucessivos

ateliês herdeiros de Picasso

pagaram impostos com desenhos

Derain Cézanne Matisse Seurat

Contra um fundo de azul mútuo

Picasso—mulher com orelha

grande e a cabeça de Fernande

Pábulo de vermes Picasso

colecionava Picuá de barro

decorado com cabra

Picasso cavado com camisa

de listas. Testa olhos nariz

e morena boca de Françoise

Gilot

o arco de sobrancelhas marca

os olhos claros (quadris largos)

pétalas de fina fêmeaflor

Em Horta de Ebro Tarragona

Boulevard de Clichy Cadaqués

Picasso e Braque em Céret Eva Gouel

The Disorder Of

The disorder of successive

ateliers Picasso's heirs

paid taxes with drawings

Derain Cézanne Matisse Seurat

Against a backdrop of reciprocal blue

Picasso—woman with large

ear and Fernande's head

Passel of worms Picasso

collected Pitcher of clay

decorated with she-goat

hollowed-out Picasso with striped

shirt. Forehead eyes nose

and olive mouth of Françoise

Gilot

the arch of eyebrows highlights

the clear eyes (large hips)

petals of slender femaleflower

the Garden of Ebro Tarragona

Boulevard de Clichy Cadaqués

Picasso and Braque in Céret Eva Gouel

Putas de Aviñón vaso, garrafa

jornais e a cor das letras kou

Boulevard Raspail Stein Sorgues

(e as futuras luas de Eluárd)

Eva morre de tuberculose

Roma Montrouge Olga Koklova

Derain no front e a "Guitarra" sem corda

Picasso propôs um diálogo

entre o espaço e a luz

(from *Ossos de Borboleta,* 1996)

Whores of Avignon vase, carafe

newspapers and the color of the letters kou

Boulevard Raspail Stein Sorgues

(and Eluard's future moons)

Eva dies from tuberculosis

Rome Montrouge Olga Koklova

Derain at the front and the stringless "Guitar"

Picasso proposed a dialogue

between space and light

—Translated from the Portuguese by Michael Palmer

Folhas

Folhas fêmeas da mandrágora
mandrágoras do agora quando
abutres habitam
azuis

bocas mais suaves do que
vinho
o sol de janeiro queima
a pele

ouriços trucidam víboras
salamandras e consoantes
sob o musgo
de cifras

(como se diz
não se adia
a cor
da noite)

camaleões
o casco oco de um cervo
lacraias mancas
a cauda de um pavão emérito

(from *Ossos de Borboleta*, 1996)

Leaves

Female mandrake leaves
mandrakes of this moment when
vultures inhabit
the blue

mouths softer than
wine
january sun burns
the skin

burs slay vipers
salamanders and consonants
under the moss
of ciphers

(as they say
the color
of night
can't be delayed)

chameleons
hollow hoof of deer
maimed centipedes
tail of an illustrious peacock

—Translated from the Portuguese by Michael Palmer

Quadrado

(para Bruna)

Uma formiga
picando nuvens
formigas traçam

trilhas quadradas
enquanto brancas
nuvens passam

o pôr-do-sol
e as girafas
de quatro em quatro

(from *Ossos de Borboleta,* 1996)

Quadrate

(to Bruna)

One ant
cropping clouds
ants trace

quadrate paths
while white
clouds pass

the sunset
giraffes
four by four

> —*Translated from the Portuguese by the author, with revisions by Robert Creeley*

Me Transformo

Me transformo,
outra janela—
outro
que se afasta e não se reaproxima

nas desobjetivações e reativações,
nas linhas e realinhamentos
outros
me atravessam

morto de ser
coisas perdem sentido
expressões figuradas como
ossos de borboleta

me transformo
na observação
de uma pétala

*

Me destransformo
a mesma janela—
outro
que não se afasta

Nas objetivações
alinhamentos
e linhas inexistentes
iguais me repassam

Retrato desativado
taxidermista de mim mesmo

(from *Ossos de Borboleta,* 1996)

I Transform Myself

I transform myself,
another window—
another
withdrawing and not returning

in disobjectivations and reactivations,
in lines and realignments
others
traverse me

dead of being
things lose sense
figurative expressions
like butterfly bones

I transform myself
by observing
a petal

*

I untransform myself
the same window—
another
not withdrawing

In objectivations,
inexistent lines
and alignments
alike repassing me

Deactivated portrait,
taxidermist of myself.

—Translated from the Portuguese by Charles Perrone

Onde

Onde eu escrevo
há o ruído
do lixo da cidade depois
de recolhido
sendo triturado

há um abajur
uma cômoda
com espelho
e uma cama
desarrumada

o outono está próximo
a janela fechada

um cansaço súbito
toma conta das palavras.

NYC/29 Set/1994

(from *Ossos de Borboleta*, 1996)

O Agapanto

O agapanto se lança em janeiro alamanda talvez canto de magnólia branca mil folhas
florena esponrinha em fevereiro manacá-março o que é flor or que é azul brinco-de-
princesa insigne em abril camélia branca de maio íris numa agulha de sol de junho
lápis-lázuli lacunas de campânulas embora chamadas de flor rododendro caliandra
que se lança jasmim ou miosótis no mês seguinte o que é sépala de outubro fulvo
antúrio cinerária petúnia jacarandá-mimoso no mês de janeiro e dezembro sálvia a
pétala deslocou a paraábola a flor secou a fáula

(from *Céu-Eclipse,* 1999)

Where

Where I write
there's the noise
of the city garbage after
it's collected
being ground

there's a lamp
a chest of drawers
with a mirror
and a bed
unmade

autumn is near
the window closed

a sudden fatigue
takes charge of the words.

NYC/Sept 29 /1994

—*Translated from the Portuguese by John Milton*

The Agapanthus

The agapanthus blooms in january yellow bell perhaps song of magnolia white milfoil
yarrow floret larkspur in february manaca-march that which is flower which is blue
princess-jewels eminent in april white amelia of may iris in a needle of june sun lapis-
lazuli lacuna of campanulas though called flower rhododendron calliandra which
blooms jasmin or myosotis on the following month which is sepal in october tawny
snapdragon cineraria petunia jacaranda-tendergrass in january and december saliva
the petal plucked the parable the flower dried the fable

—*Translated from the Portuguese by Jennifer Sarah Frota*

171196

1

Nunca morei numa rua chamada Vidro. Chutei uma
vez paralelepípedos. Cada dia passava como se num
espelho—de ecos. Telefones, fios. Uma vez andei de
barco num lago. Nunca me vi em meu próprio
reflexo. Falas, conversas—uma só figura e pessoa.
Alto-falante mudo. Também morei num aparta-
mento minúsculo. Gosto do nome das ruas
de alguns amigos. Amherst, Mílvia, Sírius. Não
tenho tempo para nada. Meus cabelos caíram. Tal-
vez isto seja tudo.

2

Meus antepassados vieram da Itália. Sicília. Nápo-
les. Veneza. Alessandro Bonvicino — Il Moretto.
Também de Pontevedra, na Galícia. Meus antepas-
sados, de mãe, vieram de minas. Meu nome: meu pai
tirou de um cartão de visita .

3

Nunca passei por uma rua chamada Tesoura. Uma
lacraia se move, por atalhos. Formigas caindo no olho.
Giuliano Della Casa, água e tinta, gosta dos quadros
de Alessandro Bonvicino. Giuliano vive em Modena,
via Sant' Agostino, 33. Passei alguns anos fechado,
aqui mesmo, num quatro. Há uma rua chamada
Tesoura. Inhambu é o nome de um pássaro. Gosto
de tomar aspirinas e hipnóticos. Uma onda de luz
me abandona agora — como a um fósforo, antes de
partir. Há um sol e uma lua, ao mesmo tempo, no
Boulevard Wilshire. Sabine Macher mora no 7 bis
rue de Paradis. Alguém mora na Legion Dr. O pneu
da bicleta não é um círculo. Há uma avenida chama-
da Precita. O céu, ontem, estava oblíquo.

171196

I

I have never lived on a street named Glass. Once I
kicked crosswalks. Each day passed as in a mirror—
echoes. Telephones, wires. Once I took a boat out on
a lake. I've never seen myself in my reflection. Words,
conversations—only one character, one person.
Megaphone mute. I've also lived in a miniscule
apartment. I like the name of the streets of some of
my friends. Amherst, Milvia, Sirius. I don't have time
for anything. My hair fell out. Maybe this is it.

2

My ancestors came from Italy. Sicily. Naples, Venice.
Alessandro Bonvicino.—Il Moretto. Also from
Pontevedra in Galicia. My maternal ancestors came
from mines. My name: my father took it from a
business card.

3

I've never run across a street named Scissors. A
centipede moves sideways. Ants fall in the eye.
Giuliano Della Casa, water and paint, likes the
paintings of Alessandro Bonvicino. Guiliano lives
in Modena, Santa Agostino Street 33. I spent some
years, right here, closed up in a room. There is a street
called Scissors. Inhambu is the name of a bird. I like
to take asprin and opiates. A light wave abandons
me now—as a match, before leaving. There is a sun
and a moon, all at once, on Wilshire Boulevard.
Sabine Macher lives at 7 Paradise Street. Somebody
lives on Legion Drive. The bicycle tire is not a circle.
There is an avenue called Precita. The sky, yesterday,
was overcast.

4

Vejo você mais tarde. O filho de onze anos de David gosta de selos estranhos. Alguém está fazendo *garage sale,* neste momento. Não senti uma queixa abafada na docilidade das flores, esta manhã. Também não vi um pássaro esguio, comendo insetos, esta manhã. Alguém mora em Gumtree Terrace. A água corre para o mar. A lua não fica cheia em um dia. Há uma rua cchamada Lepic. Há uma outra, Lindero Nuevo Vedado. Aquela calçada está suja. Sweet William é o nome de uma flor. Elefantes não fiam pontas de agulha.

5

Talvez tenha morado numa rua chamada *Sí dar.* Há uma rua chamada Campeche. Rose e Andy moram com certeza na Cedar Street. Maçãs não significam nada. Dizem que existe um sedativo especial para lesmas. Ninguém explica certas expansões do verde. Árvores grandes não dão frutos, apenas sombra. Sequóias e conchas enlouquecem os homens. Uma mulher esmerilha, pelo telefone. Há uma rua chamada Cedro. Cilícios consentem dias e arames. Estátuas
                fazem parte
                        do
                                universo

(from *Sky-Eclipse,* 2000)

4

I'll see you later. David's eleven year old son likes
foreign stamps. At this very moment, someone is
having a *garage sale*. I didn't feel like complaining for
the docileness of flowers this morning. I also didn't
see a thin bird, eating insects, this morning. Someone
lives on Gumtree Terrace. The water runs to the sea.
The moon doesn't fill in during day. There is a street
called Lepic. There is another, Lindero Nuevo Ve-
dado. That sidewalk is dirty. Sweet William is the
name of a flower. Elephants don't thread needles.

5

Perhaps I have lived on a street called *Si Dar*. There is
a street called Campeche. Rose and Andy, certainly,
live on Cedar Street. Apples mean nothing. They
say that a special sedative exists for snails. Nobody
explains certain expanses of green. Large trees don't
bear fruit, just shade. Sequoias and shells drive men
insane. A woman investigates by phone. There is a
street called Cedro. Cecilia senses the millennia and
wires. Statues
          are part
              of the
                   universe

—*Translated from the Portuguese by Jennifer Sarah Frota, Scott Bentley,
and Douglas Messerli*

Angela de Campos
1960

Born in Rio de Janeiro on January 1st, 1960, Angela de Campos completed her courses in literary studies at the Federal University of Rio de Janeiro (AFRJ) and at the Catholic University of Rio de Janeiro. Married to a diplomat, she has lived in several cities, among them Mexico City. She is now living in Madrid. More recently, her poetry has appeared in the anthology of Brazilian poetry *Pinorama / 30 poetas brasileiros.*

BOOKS OF POETRY:

Feixe de Lontras (Rio de Janeiro: Livraria Sette Letras, 1996)

A corcova calva do camelo
me traz o desejo
de incendiar as vogais
e ruminar as cinzas arenosas.

Como a alma acalma o coração?
Talvez com dromedários.

(from *Feixe de Lontras*, 1996)

A tarde se estira
no dorso de um tigre
veloz—
o duro mel dos olhos
encorpa em camélias
súbitas esquinas sem beijos,—
todos os minutos se espreitam.

(from *Feixe de Lontras*, 1996)

O tempo soluça no relógio
as rugas horizontais
que não tatuam meu rosto.
Ponteiros
agulhas invisíveis
injetam o ritmo
que infecta o dia.

(from *Feixe de Lontras*, 1996)

The camel's bald hump
wakes my desire
to burn the vowels
and chew the gritty ashes.

How does the soul soothe the heart?
Maybe with dromedaries.

—Translated from the Portuguese by Michael Palmer

Afternoon stretches out
on the back of a swift
tiger—
the hard honey of the eyes
thickens into camellias
sudden corners without kisses,—
all the minutes spy on each other.

—Translated from the Portuguese by Michael Palmer

Time hiccups from the clock
the horizontal wrinkles
that don't tattoo my face
Invisible needles
its hands
inject the rhythm
that infects the day

—Translated from the Portuguese by Michael Palmer

Age de Carvalho
1958

Carvalho was born in Belém, in the Pará state of Brazil in 1958. He majored in architecture and is now a graphic designer by profession. His books include *Arquitetura dos Ossos* (1980), *A fala entre parênteses* (1982), *Arena, areia* (1986), and *Ror* (1990). He currently lives in Vienna, Austria.

BOOKS OF POETRY:

Arquitetura de Ossos (Belém: Editora Falângola/Semec, 1980); *A fala entre parênteses* (Belém: Edições Grapho/Gráfica Semec, 1982); *Arena, areia* (Belém: Grafisa/Edições Grapho, 1986); *Ror* (São Paulo: Duas Cidades, Secretaria de Estado da Cultura, 1990)

Passagem

Era julho
floresciam pedras
carregavas a sombra de um rio

Chamavam-nos
agosto, norte, ninguém

Irreconciliáveis

(from *Ror*)

Negativo de Ricardo Reis

Bocas roxas (não
de vinho),
sobre a testa
branca cresce a erva

Não te chamo Lídia : nada
sabemos sobre o rio das coisas

(from *Ror*)

A Idade Do Carvalho

A idade do carvalho
aflora real na pedra
(ágrafo círculo da pedra,
a sombra e a diferença)
aponta para o deserto,
declina
       o ramo do nome
onde espera uma data,
a resposta

(from *Ror*)

Passage

It was July
stones were blooming
you hauled the river's shadow

We were called:
august, north, nobody

Irreconcilable.

—Translated from the Portuguese by Dana Stevens

Negative of Ricardo Reis

Mouths purple (not
with wine),
above the white
brow grass grows

I don't call you Lydia: we know
nothing of the river of things

—Translated from the Portuguese by Dana Stevens

The Age of the Oak

The age of the oak
blossoms from stone
(unwritten circle of stone,
shadow and difference)
points to the desert,
inflects
          the branch of a name,
awaits a date,
the answer

—Translated from the Portuguese by the author

a Monika Grond

A C U R A, e a sua aura
esvaziada de abismo

O abismo—o íntimo
    ascender

um estrelar-se infinito
    (de boca
contra) ao beijo cru
da queda

(from *Ror*)

for Monika Grond

The C U R E, and its emptied
air of abyss

The abyss—the intimate
          ascending

an infinite starring
          (of mouth
against) the raw kiss
of falling

   —Translated from the Portuguese by Dana Stevens

Ana Cristina Cesar
1952-1983

Born in 1952 in Rio de Janeiro, Cesar wrote for news-
papers and alternative journals in the 1970s. She was
also active in journalism, television and literary re-
search. Her published books of the period include
*Nada esta espuma; Cenas de abril; Correspondência
Completa;* and *Luvas de Pelica,* collected under the
title *A teus pés* in 1982. On October 29, 1983, Cesar
committed suicide, apparently as a result of her
sexual involvements in Rio de Janeiro during the
Military Dictatorship.

Several of her manuscripts were collected after her
death as *Escritos da Inglaterra* in 1985. Her posthu-
mous work also includes the book of poetry *Inéditos
e Dispersos.*

BOOKS OF POETRY:

Nada esta espuma; Cenas de abril (Rio de Janeiro: Edição do autor, 1970); *Correspondência
Completa; Luvas de Pelica: A teus pés* (São Paulo: Editora Brasilense, 1982); *Inéditos e Dispersos*
(São Paulo: Editora Brasilense, 1985)

Sumário

Polly Kellog e o motorista Osmar.
Dramas rápidos mas intensos.
Fotogramas do meu coração conceitual.
De tomara-que-caia azul marinho.
Engulo desaforos mas com sinceridade.
Sonsa com bom-senso.
Antena da praça.
Artista da poupança.
Absolutely blind.
Tesão do talvez.
Salta-pocinhas.
Água na boca.
Anjo que registra.

(from *A teus pés*, 1982)

Nada, Esta Espuma

Por afrontamento do desejo
insisto na maldade de escrever
mas não sei se a deusa sobe à superfície
ou apenas me castiga com seus uivos.
Da amurada deste barco
quero tanto os seios da sereia

(from *A teus pés*, 1982)

A história está completa: *wide sargasso sea*, azul
azul que não me espanta, e canta como uma
sereia de papel.

(from *A teus pés*, 1982)

Summary

Polly Kellogg and the chauffeur Osmar.
Rapid but intense dramas.
Photo romances of the conceptual heart.
Of the navy blue strapless dress.
I swallow insults but with sincerity.
Giddy with good sense.
Aerial of the square.
Artist of savings.
Absolutely blind.
Lust for the perhaps.
Mincing gait.
Water in my mouth.
An angel that registers.

—*Translated from the Portuguese by John Milton*

Nothing, This Foam

To confront desire
I insist on the evil of writing
but I don't know if the goddess comes up to the surface
or if she just punishes me with her howls.
From the bulwarks of this boat
how I long for the mermaid's breasts.

—*Translated from the Portuguese by John Milton*

The story is complete: wide sargasso sea, blue
blue that doesn't frighten me, and sings like a
paper mermaid.

—*Translated from the Portuguese by John Milton*

é muito claro
amor
bateu
para ficar
nesta varanda descoberta
a anoitecer sobre a cidade
em construção
sobre a pequena constrição
no teu peito
angústia de felicidade
luzes de automóveis
riscando o tempo
canteiros de obras
em repouso
recuo súbito da trama

(from *A teus pés*, 1982)

Quando entre nós só havia
uma carta certa
a correspondência
completa
o trem os trilhos
a janela aberta
uma certa paisagem
sem pedras ou
sobressaltos
meu salto alto
em equilíbrio
o copo d'água
a espera do café

(from *A teus pés*, 1982)

it's very clear
love is here
to stay
on this open veranda
night falls over the city
under construction
on the small constriction
on your breast
anguish of happiness
car headlights
slashing time
road works
at rest
a sudden recoil from the plot

—*Translated from the Portuguese by John Milton*

When between us there was just
a letter certain to come
complete
correspondence
the train the tracks
the window open
a certain landscape
without stones or
alarms
my high heel
balancing
the glass of water
the wait for coffee

—*Translated from the Portuguese by John Milton*

Traveling

Tarde da noite recoloco a casa toda em seu
lugar.
Guardo os papéis todos que sobraram.
Confirmo para mim a solidez dos cadeados.
Nunca mais te disse uma palavra.
Do alto da serra de Petrópolis,
com um chapéu de ponta e um regador,
Elizabeth confirmava, "Perder
é mais fácil que se pensa."
Rasgo os papéis todos que sobraram.
"Os seus olhos pecam, mas seu corpo
não," dizia o tradutor preciso, simultâneo,
e suas mãos é que tremiam. "… perigoso,"
ria a Carolina perita no papel Kodak.
A câmera em rasante viajava.
A voz em off nas montanhas, inextinguível
fogo domado da paixão, a voz
do espelho dos meus olhos,
negando-se a todas as viagens,
e a voz rascante da velocidade,
de todas três bebi um pouco
sem notar
como quem procura um fio.
Nunca mais te disse
uma palavra, repito, preciso alto,
tarde da noite,
enquanto desalinho
sem luxo
sede
agulhadas
os pareceres que ouvi num dia interminável:
sem parecer mais com a luz ofuscante desse
　　　　　　　　　mesmo dia interminável

(from *A teus pés*, 1982)

Traveling

Late at night I put the whole house back in its
place.
I put all the leftover papers away.
I make sure of the soundness of the locks.
I never said another word to you.
From the top of the hills of Petrópolis,
with a pointed hat and a watering can,
Elizabeth confirmed, "The art of losing
isn't hard to master."
I rip up the leftover paper.
"Your eyes sin, but your body
doesn't," said the precise, simultaneous translator,
and it was his hands that trembled. "It's dangerous,"
laughed the skilled Carolina on Kodak paper.
The lowdown camera panned.
The voiceover in the hills, indestructible
tamed fire of passion, the voice
of the mirror of my eyes
denying all the journeys,
and the shrill voice of speed,
I drank a little of all three
without noticing
like someone looking for a thread.
I never said another word to you,
I repeat, I state firmly,
late at night
while I lose direction
with no luxury
thirst
pricks
the seemings I heard in an endless day:
without seeming more like the dazzling light of this
                    same interminable day

—*Translated from the Portuguese by John Milton*

Horácio Costa
1954

REGINA STELLA

Born in São Paulo in 1954, Costa pursued his studies in Brazil and the United States. He earned a B.A. degree from the University of São Paulo in 1978 and a M.A. from New York University in 1983. He received a PhD from Yale University in 1994.

For a long while Costa lived in Mexico City, where he was a professor at the National Autonomous University of Mexico (UNAM); but in the past few years he has returned to live in São Paulo.

Costa's poetry evinces a high wit and a strong visual texture, along with his active concerns for the rights of homosexuals. Among his many book publications are *28 poemas 6 contos* (1981), *Satori* (1989), *O livro dos fracta* (1990), *The very short stories* (1991), *Los jardines y los poetas* (a bilingual Spanish-Portuguese anthology, 1993), *O menino e o travesseiro* (1994), and *Quadragésimo*, published in 1998. In addition to extensive critical writing, Costa has translated the poetry of authors such as Elizabeth Bishop and Octavio Paz.

BOOKS OF POETRY:

28 poemas, 6 contos (São Paulo: José Gatti, 1981); *Satori* (São Paulo: Iluminuras, 1989); *O livro dos fracta* (São Paulo: Iluminuras, 1990); *Quadragésimo* (São Paulo: Ateliê Editorial, 1998)

ENGLISH LANGUAGE TRANSLATIONS:

Selected poems in *Quadragésimo* (São Paulo: Ateliê, 1998); poems in "Lies About the Truth: An Anthology of Brazilian Poetry," edited by Régis Bonvicino in collaboration with Tarso M. de Melo, in *New American Writing*, no 18 (2000).

VIII
Zona

Não conte o número. Sem primeira nem última, as ondas do mar. Fragmentos:
diante dos palmeirais, um rebanho lentíssimo. Vêm vêm vêm. Calmaria é
dos zebus o mascar indefinido. Exegi monumentum aere perennius. Tantalizing.

(from *O livro dos fracta*, 1990)

XV
Buraco Negro

O animal enfurecido engole seus próprios halos. Negra a cor
da luz interna. O quase, sua máscara. Ouvimos seus queixumes
de anjo omnívoro. No quarto, às escuras, penso em meu pai.

(from *O livro dos fracta*, 1990)

XXI

Qual a área que esconde a liberdade de uma linha?
relacionam-se universos do plano ao monte, arfam pulsares pelos
interstícios. Se te aprouver, inscreve tua fractalidade na pele do papel.

(from *O livro dos fracta*, 1990)

XLV
A Tentação De Santo Antônio

no céu a terceira Visão perscruta ornitorrincos monstruosos
no coração cabeça o V do eVangelho rói a moldura do menino antigo
debaixo de meus pés *the breaking of the Vessels* os ratos absolutos a absolVição

(from *O livro dos fracta*, 1990)

VIII
Zone

Don't count the number. No first or last, the waves of the sea. Fragments:
  before the palm groves, how slow the flock. They come come come. Calm is
zebra's indefinite chewing. Exegi monumentum aere perennius. Tantalizing.

—*Translated from the Portuguese by Charles Perrone*

XV
Black Hole

The furious animal swallows its own halos. Black the color
  of the inner light. An almost, its mask. We heard its angelic
omnivorous complaints. In the darkness of the room, I think of my father.

—*Translated from the Portuguese by Charles Perrone*

XXI

What space can hide the liberty of a line?
From mountains to plains universes relate, pulsars heave and pant
in interstices. If it please thee, inscribe thy fractality on paper's skin.

—*Translated from the Portuguese by Charles Perrone*

XLV
The Temptation of Saint Anthony

in the heavens the third Vision examines monstrous ornithorhyncus
in the head heart the V of eVangelism gnaws the frame of the ancient boy
under my feet the breaking of the Vessels the absolute rats absolVing

—*Translated from the Portuguese by Charles Perrone*

O Retrato de Dom Luís de Góngora

cara de vampiro, nariz boxeado pela vida,
stiffness, teu legendário orgulho desmesurado,
sem ironia ou sorriso a boca nos cantos desce,
não vejo tuas mãos, estarão escrevendo,
estarão manipulando o ábaco da sintaxe,
preocupado te vejo em encontrar tesouros
dormentes, na folha branca brilham larvais,
e já fixos me perfuram teus olhos de esfinge,
que imitam tuas orelhas em leque, teu manteau
absoluto, mole de lã ou veludo, sempre Diretor
dum hospital barroco antes do Grand Renfermement,
para quem posas, cantas o Esgueva do pensamento
de teus contemporâneos, o radical suspiro da Natureza
em cio profundo, linguagem láctea, campo blau,
e me avalias, por fora Ácis, por dentro Polifemo.
assim é o mundo Dom Luís, para mim estás posando,
pré-kafkiana barata insigne vai de ante em ante-sala,
paciente expõe seu elástico decoro enfático, tanto
tens que suportar, por fora Hyde, por dentro tão menino,
pois és menino e más allá da moldura deste quadro
como os negros falas—é de noite que em pérola
se transforma a banalidade, e tua calva preenche
o céu, cede o vazio, e tua palavra uma berceuse escapa.

México, 1984

(from *Satori*, 1989)

Portrait of Don Luís de Gôngora

vampire face, life-battered nose,
stiffness your immoderate pride,
the corners of your smile drawn down without irony,
I do not see your hands, they might be writing,
they might be manipulating syntax's abacus,
I see you absorbed in seeking dormant treasures,
larvae shimmer on the white page,
and your sphinx eyes, now fixed, penetrate me
they imitate your fan-like ears, your full cloak,
a mass of velvet or wool, Director always
of a baroque hospital before the Grand Renfermement,
for whom do you pose? you sing of the Esgueva
of your contemporaries' thought, the radical sigh
of Nature in deep heat, lacteal language, azure field,
and you value me, Acis without, Polyphemus within,
this is the world Don Luis, you are sitting for me,
distinguished pre-Kafkan cockroach goes from ante
to anteroom, patiently expounds his emphatic elastic decorum,
this much you must put up with, Jekyll without,
so small within, because you are child and beyond
the canvas' frame you speak as blacks do—it is at night
that banality becomes a pearl, and your baldness fills the sky,
the void yields, and a lullaby escapes your word.

México, 1984

—Translated from the Portuguese by Martha Black Jordan

História Natural

Detrás do taxidermista, há a palha,
detrás do rinoceronte, a savana,
detrás desta escritura só a noite,
a noite que galopa até o fronte.

Na asa da mariposa assoma a lua,
na cabeça do alfinete brilha o sol,
nestas linhas reverbera um sol negro,
o astro que ora sobe no horizonte.

O animal dissecado da sintaxe
provê o verbo, o bastidor e a legenda
duma coleção mais morta que os mortos.

No gabinete de história natural
o visitante-leitor detém-se face
a mamíferos e insetos reluzentes.

(from *Quadragésimo*, 1998)

Natural History

Behind the taxidermist, there's the straw,
behind the rhinoceros, the savannah,
behind this writing only the night,
night which gallops to the fore.

The moon leaps from the butterfly's wing,
the sun shines on the head of a pin,
a black sun thrums through these lines,
star now rising on the horizon.

The dessicated animal of syntax
furnishes the word, the frame and the label
of a collection deader than the dead.

In the natural history collection
the visiting reader pauses alongside
shining mammals and insects.

—*Translated from the Portuguese by Martha Black Jordan*

Canções do Muro

1

Quem botou o reboco neste muro
não tinha o domínio de espátula,
ignorava a mescla correta da argamassa,
não era bom pedreiro.

Ou será o tempo apenas o culpado
pela destruição do seu trabalho?
Não faz assim tantos anos
que leventaram este muro.

Pintaram-no de branco
e várias vezes repintaram-no,
de branco primeiro, depois só de tons ocres.

2

O sol batia e pino sobre o muro
que parecia estar ali
desde que é o mundo mundo:
os passantes não o percebiam mais.

Usaram-no como suporte
de campanhas políticas & publicitárias,
Kolinos & logos
& siglas & partidos
impressos com tinta barata.

Songs of the Wall

1

Whoever applied plaster to this wall
wasn't handy with a trowel,
didn't know the right mixture for mortar,
wasn't a good mason.

Or is time to blame
for the destruction?
This was raised
not so long ago.

It was painted white
and repainted several times,
first white, then just tones of ochre.

2

The sun shone full on the wall
which seemed to have been there
ever since the world, world:
passersby no longer took note.

It was used as a stage
for political & ad campaigns
Kolynos & logos
& acronyms & factions
printed in cheap ink.

3

Usaram-no também para grafites:
escreveram sobre rostos & restos
de affiches & argamassa
como se sobre uma folha em branco.

Virou a carne do muro
uma espécie de pasta: um Tàpies
esquecido num canto de cidade, obra in progress
de significado igual & forma instável
(do lado de lá, escondia-se /
esconde-se
o velho jardim de rosas).

4

Quem reparou na progressão das gretas
sobre a sua superfície & mediu
a deslavagem & a erosão milimétricos?
Quem leu as pautas que se formavam?
Quem viu o reboco cair como icebergs
no oceano da calçada?

A sós se desfazia /
se desfaz o muro,
sua música para ninguém cantada,
surdina para surdos, cantochão para o chão,
nu descendo a escada numa casa vazia,
natividade num museu antártico.

3

It was used for graffiti too:
scribbled faces & scraps
of posters & mortar
as if it were a blank page.

The flesh of the wall became
a sort of paste: a Tàpies
forgotten in some corner of the city, a work in progress
of equal significance & unstable form
(on the other side, was hidden /
is hidden
the old garden of roses).

4

Who noticed the growing cracks
on its surface & measured
the fading & the kilometrical erosion?
Who read the score that took shape?
Who saw the plaster fall like icebergs
into the ocean of the sidewalk?

The wall was collapsing /
collapses by itself,
its music sung for no one,
mute for the deaf, plainsong for the plain,
nude descending the staircase in an empty house,
nativity in an Antarctic museum.

5

Por isso cantaria eu o muro?
Por isso eximiria eu
o pedreiro do mau reboco
de seu mau trabalho
de há quarenta & mais anos?

Sua obra resultou em obra d'arte
— que vive na retina, que não no espaço —,
mas não é esta a razão,
nem este poema a sua defesa
nem a épica do descobrimento súbito
do muro.

6

Canto o muro porque sim,
porque sua pele & a minha se assemelham
posto que também já tomei sol & tomei chuva,
posto que sobre o meu corpo discursos
& campanhas se imprimiram /
imprimi:
já tive tantas caras & sorri
como foram da minha vida os meses
& as idéias políticas ou não
que se sobrepuseram
umas sobre as outras

5

For that shall I sing of the wall?
For that shall I absolve
the mason from shoddy mortar
his shoddy workmanship
of some forty years ago?

His work resulted in a work of art
— which lives in the retina, not in space —
but this is not the reason,
nor this poem his defense
nor the epic of the sudden discovery
of the wall.

6

I sing the wall just
because its skin resembles mine
since I too have been under the sun & beneath the rain,
since on my body speeches
& campaigns were printed /
I printed:
I had as many faces & smiles
as there were months of my life
& ideas, political or not,
which have layered themselves
one atop another

7

Canto-o & dou-lhe olhos & ouvidos
para cantar-me a mim;
ao emprestar-lhe minha voz /
tomá-lo emprestado para a minha voz
Eu canto a mim.

edificado por acaso numa esquina do tempo
(do outro lado, o velho jardim de rosas)
ruminando, cantarolando o que me apraz
(sim que há rosas, me disseram)

& os Tàpies, os topázios
sobre a minha pele
(& as pétalas)

8

& as fraturas
& os desmoronamentos
& as cantigas da gravidade
& o caminho ao pó

o meu caminho
& o muro.

(previously unpublished)

7

I sing of it & give it eyes & ears
to sing of me;
when I loan it my voice /
borrow it for my voice
I sing of myself,

built by chance on a corner of time
(on the other side, the old garden of roses)
ruminating, humming whatever pleases me
(yes there are roses, I have been told)

& Tàpies, the topazes
on my skin
(& the petals)

8

& the fractures
& the crumbling
& the canticles of gravity
& the road toward dust

my road
& the wall

—Translated from the Portuguese by Martha Black Jordan

Júlio Castañon Guimarães
1951

Guimarães was born in 1951. Among his books of poetry are *Vertentes* (1975), *17 peças* (1983), and *Inscrições* (1992). He has translated Francis Ponge, Gertrude Stein, Roland Barthes, George Steiner, Mallarmé, Valéry, and Michel Butor, and also written an important essay on the Brazilian writer Murilo Mendes, *Territórios/conjunções: posias e prosa críticas de Murilo Mendes*. He was the editor of the critical edition of *Crônica da casa assassinada* by Lucio Cardoso (1991), and co-edited the critical edition of Manuel Bandeira's poems. He currently works as a researcher at Casa Rui Barbosa in Rio de Janeiro.

BOOKS OF POETRY:

Vertentes (Rio de Janeiro: Edição do autor, 1975); *17 peças* (Rio de Janeiro: Edição do author, 1983); *Inscrições* (Rio de Janeiro: Imago, 1992); *Dois poemas estrangeiros* (Ouro Preto: Tipografia do Fundo de Ouro Preto, 1995); *Matéria e Paisagem e poemas anteriores* (Rio de Janeiro: Sette Letras, 1998)

ENGLISH LANGUAGE TRANSLATIONS:

Selected poems in "Lies About the Truth: An Anthology of Brazilian Poetry," edited by Régis Bonvicino in collaboration with Tarso M. de Melo, in *New American Writing*, no. 18 (2000).

Geografia

sombras ancestrais
claras manhãs
em que margem?
ainda que a memória esbata as horas
o que há são espaços perdidos
uma casa
uma viagem
cabelos soltos em minhas mãos

(from *Vertentes*, 1975)

Sem Título, Óleo Sobre Tela, 70 x 50 cm

quando, desfeitos os
nós da representação,
contra si a imagem
investe, pouco resta
além da indagação
cínica ou retórica:
que imagem elide
sua crua corrupção?

(from *Inscrições*, 1992)

Geography

ancestral shadows
bright mornings
what margin?
while memory dilutes the hours
what there are are lost spaces
a house
a trip
hair unbound in my hands

—*Translated from the Portuguese by Dana Stevens*

Untitled, Oil on Canvas, 70 x 50 cm

when, the knots of
representation undone,
the image weighs
against itself, little is left
beyond cynical
or rhetorical inquiry:
what image annuls
this raw corruption?

—*Translated from the Portuguese by Dana Stevens*

O Que Se Perdeu?

os cabelos de teu peito
nas tardes de domingo

nenhuma imagem
nenhuma estratégia

perdeu-se este poema
nu ardorosamente nu
e vivo e aceso
na ponta da língua

por entre tuas pernas

(from *Inscrições*, 1992)

No horizonte, irresoluções. As tentativas cumulam incer-
tezas, mas mesmo pontuações (talvez) sem propósito de-
senham ritmos; organizam-se séries de razões equívocas e
desatenções; destroços de procedimentos, de exigências e
de métodos emergem : mal disfarçado rigor resiste—ma-
téria, trama, viagem, diário.

(from *Inscrições*, 1992)

What Was Lost?

the hairs of your chest
on sunday afternoons

no image
no strategy

this poem was lost
naked, ardently naked
alive and lit
on the tongue's tip

between your legs

—Translated from the Portuguese by Dana Stevens

On the horizon, irresolutions. Attempts accumulate uncer-
tainties, but even pointless (perhaps) punctuations sketch
rhythms; set up series of dubious reasons and
inattentions; expose the wreckage of procedures, requirements
and methods: barely disguised, rigor resists—matter,
plot, journey, journal.

—Translated from the Portuguese by Dana Stevens

Última Canção

Como esquecer a noite crivada de estrelas, cravada fundo no destempero? Se o céu se abria adiante, abrigando o alcance do olhar, todas as penhas e o cenário de adornos.

Por uma mínima trilha de Minas, entre capins e capelas, era possível erguer não a voz, não o tranco, mas a espera. Que avançava, alerta, pelas curvas de cada pausa. Que sabia, pelas margens, aonde ainda não se chegava. Embora o hálito de músculos tesos, embora o tato sem controle, embora súbito vagas de dissolução.

(Alguns ruídos de insetos, carrapichos na barra da calça, latidos ao longe.) Vertigem de fumos no ar enregelado ou tentativas de ardor desfeitas por uma lógica em precipício não desvendarão, sequer sujarão, as miúdas cifras interpostas entre o quase entrelaçamento.

Aqui mais vasto podia ser o pasmo, mais vasto podia ser o avesso. Sem cismas, assim como sem resignações. Rente ao chão, sentindo no corpo a terra úmida de sereno.

(from *Matéria e Paisagem*, 1998)

Last Song

How to forget the night perforated with stars, penetrated deep into the disorder? If the sky opened up ahead, sheltering the reach of sight, all the cliffs and the decorated setting.

On a narrow trail in Minas, between grass and chapels, it was possible to increase not the voice, not the trot, only the anticipation. Which advanced, alert, through curves of each pause. Which knew, by the banks, where it had yet to arrive. Despite the scent of taut muscles, despite the uncontrolable stuttering, despite sudden waves of dissolution.

(Sounds of insects, burrs stuck to the pant-leg hem, barking in the distance). Swirls of smoke in the frozen air or attempts at ardor undone by a logic on the precipice they won't reveal, not even soil, the small ciphers located between the almost interlacement.

Here vaster could be the wonder, vaster could be the reverse. Without illusions, as without reservations. Close to the ground, the body feeling the earth humid with dew.

—Translated from the Portuguese by Jennifer Sarah Frota

Paulo Leminski
1945-1989

Born in Curitiba on August 24, 1945, Paulo Leminski led a life on the margins of society, working in advertisitng and intermittent collaboration with newspapers and journals. Leminski died in 1989 from alcohol abuse. Despite the difficulties of his life, he wrote several works of prose fiction and poetry. Among his works of prose are *Catatau* (1975), *Agora é que são elas* (1986), and *Metamorfose* (1994, posthumously published). His poetry books include *Quarenta Cliques em Curtiba* (1979), *Polonaise* (1980), *Caprichos e Relaxos* (1983), *Distraídos Venceremos* (1987), and *La vie en close* (1991, published posthumously). He also wrote critical works, including *Basho* (1983), *Leon Trotski, a paixão segundo a revolução* (1986), *Cruz e Souz* (1983), and *Anseios críticos* (1986). He is now recognized as one of the most important poets of his generation.

BOOKS OF POETRY:

Quarenta Cliques em Curtiba (1979); *Polonaise* (1980); *Caprichos e Relaxos* (São Paulo: Editora Brasiliense, 1983), *Distraídos Venceremos* (1987); *La vie en close* (São Paulo: Editora Brasiliense, 1991)

ENGLISH LANGUAGE TRANSLATIONS:

Selected poems in "Lies About the Truth: An Anthology of Brazilian Poetry," edited by Régis Bonvicino in collaboration with Tarso M. de Melo, in *New American Writing*, no. 18 (2000)

Pelo

pelo
branco
magnólia

o
azul
manhã
vermelho
olha

(from *Caprichos e Relaxos*, 1983)

O Assassino Era O Escriba

Meu professor de análise sintática era o tipo do sujeito
inexistente.
Um pleonasmo, o principal predicado de sua vida,
regular como um paradigma da la conjugação.
Entre uma oração subordinada e um adjunto
adverbial, ele não tinha dúvidas: sempre achava um jeito
assindético de nos torturar com um aposto.
Casou com uma regência.
Foi infeliz.
Era possessivo como um pronome.
E ela era bitransitiva.
Tentou ir para os E U A.
Não deu.
Acharam um artigo indefinido em sua bagagem.
A interjeição do bigode declinava partículas expletivas,
conectivos e agentes da passiva, o tempo todo.
Um dia, matei-o com um objeto direto na cabeça.

(from *Caprichos e Relaxos*, 1983)

Through

through
magnolia
white

the
morning
blue
sees
red

—Translated from the Portuguese by Michael Palmer

The Assassin Was the Scribe

My professor of syntactical analysis was a sort of
nonexistent subject.
A pleonasm, principal predicate of your life,
common as a paradigm of conjugation.
Between subordinated oration and adverbial
adjunct he had no doubts: always found an
asyndetic way to torture us with an appositive.
He married grammatical rectitude.
Was unhappy.
Was possessive like a pronoun.
And she was bitransitive.
He tried to go to the USA.
No way.
They discovered an indefinite article in his suitcase.
His moustache's exclamation point declined explicatives,
connectives and passives, forever.
One day I greased him with a direct object through the head.

—Translated from the Portuguese by Michael Palmer

um dia
a gente ia ser homero
a obra nada menos que uma ilíada

depois
a barra pesando
dava pra ser aí um rimbaud
um ungaretti um fernando pessoa qualquer
um lorca um éluard um ginsberg

por fim
acabamos o pequeno poeta de província
que sempre fomos
por trás de tantas máscaras
que o tempo tratou como a flores

(from *Caprichos e Relaxos*, 1983)

o pauloleminski
é um cachorro louco
que deve ser morto
a pau a pedra
a fogo a pique
senão é bem capaz
o filhadaputa
de fazer chover
em nosso piquenique

(from *Caprichos e Relaxos*, 1983)

A quem me queima
e, queimando, reina,
    valha esta teima.
Um dia, melhor me queira.

(from *Caprichos e Relaxos*, 1983)

once
we were going to be homer
the work an iliad no less

later
things got tougher
we could maybe manage a rimbaud
an ungaretti some fernando pessoa
a lorca a ginsberg an éluard

finally
we ended up the minor provincial poet
we were always
hiding behind the many masks
time treated as flowers

—*Translated from the Portuguese by Regina Alfarano, with revisions by Robert Creeley*

pauloleminski
is a mad dog
that must be beaten to death
with a rock with a stick
by a flame by a kick
or else he might very well
the sonofabitch
spoil our picnic

—*Translated from the Portuguese by Regina Alfarano*

Whoever burns
me and, burning, reigns,
    take this game.
One day, cherish my name.

—*Translated from the Portuguese by Regina Alfarano, with revisions by Robert Creeley*

     lua à vista
brilhavas assim
     sobre auschwitz?

(from *Caprichos e Relaxos,* 1983)

    apagar-me
    diluir-me
    desmanchar-me
    até que depois
    de mim
    de nós
    de tudo
    não reste mais
    que o charme

(from *Caprichos e Relaxos,* 1983)

    nada que o sol
    não explique

    tudo que a lua
    mais chique

    não tem chuva
    que desbote essa flor

(from *Caprichos e Relaxos,* 1983)

                moon
did you shine like this
            over auschwitz?

—*Translated from the Portuguese by Regina Alfarano, with revisions by Robert Creeley*

let me vanish
let me melt
let me fall apart
until
after me
after us
after all
nothing but charm
is left

—*Translated from the Portuguese by Regina Alfarano, with revisions by Robert Creeley*

nothing the sun
could not explain

everything the moon
makes glamorous

no rain
fades this flower

—*Translated from the Portuguese by Regina Alfarano, with revisions by Robert Creeley*

um poema
que não se entende
é digno de nota

a dignidade suprema
de um navio
perdendo a rota

(from *Caprichos e Relaxos*, 1983)

Olhar Paralisador N.91

o olhar da cobra   pára

             dispara
             paralisa o pássaro

                  meu olhar
                  cai de mim
                  laser
                  luar
meu despertar   despertar
meu amor desesperado   do meu olhar
meu mau olhado   despertador
                meu olhar
                leitor

(from *Caprichos e Relaxos*, 1983)

a poem
nobody understands
is worthy of note

supreme dignity
of a wondering
boat

*—Translated from the Portuguese by Dana Stevens, with
revisions by Robert Creeley*

Paralyzing Gaze 91

the gaze of the cobra   lies

                belays
                paralyzes the bird

                    my gaze
                    falls away
                    lunar
                    laser

my awakening   to arouse
my disarming love   from my alarming
my evil eye   gaze
                  my gaze
                  reader

—Translated from the Portuguese by Charles Perrone

Dois Loucos No Bairro

um passa os dias
chutando postes para ver se acendem

o outro as noites
apagando palavras
contra um papel branco

todo bairro tem um louco
que o bairro trata bem
só falta mais um pouco
pra eu ser tratado também

(from *Caprichos e Relaxos,* 1983)

Verdura

De repente
Me lembro do verde
a cor verde
a mais verde que existe
a cor mais alegre
a cor mais triste
o verde que vestes
o verde que vestiste
no dia em que te vi
no dia em que me viste

De repente
Vendi meus filhos
a uma família americana
eles têm carro
eles têm grana
eles têm casa e a grama é bacana
Só assim eles podem voltar
e pegar um sol em Copacabana

(from *Caprichos e Relaxos,* 1983)

Two Madmen in the Neighborhood

one of them spends his days
kicking lampposts to see if they light up

the second his nights
erasing words
from white paper

every neighborhood has a madman
it takes beneath its wing
not long till I can
be treated for the same damn thing

> —Translated from the Portuguese by Regina Alfarano, with
> revisions by Dana Stevens

Greenery

Suddenly
I recall the greenness
of the color green
the greenest there has ever been
the happiest hue
that makes me blue
the green you wear
green as you were
the day I met you
and you met me too

Suddenly
I sold my kids
to an American family
they've got a van
they've got the dough
they've got a house
and their lawn is fun
when back in Rio, now they can
go to the beach and get a tan

> —Translated from the Portuguese by Nelson Ascher

Minha cabeça cortada
Joguei na tua janela
Noite de lua
Janela aberta

Bate na parede
Perdendo dentes
Cai na cama
Pesada de pensamentos

Talvez te assustes
Talvez a contemples
Contra a lua
Buscando a cor de meus olhos

Talvez a uses
Como despertador
Sobre o criado-mudo

Não quero assustar-te
Peço apenas um tratamento condigno
Para essa cabeça súbita
De minha parte

(from *Caprichos e Relaxos*, 1983)

My cut-off head
Thrown in your window
Moon-lit night
Window open

Hits the wall
Loses some teeth
Falls to the bed
Heavy with thought

Maybe it's scary
Maybe you'll blink
Seeing by moon
The color of my eyes

Maybe you'll think
It's just your alarm clock
On the nightstand

Not to scare you
Only to ask kindlier treatment
For my sudden head
Departed

*—Translated from the Portuguese by Charles Bernstein and
Régis Bonvicino*

O Bicho Alfabeto

O bicho alfabeto
tem vinte e três patas
ou quase

por onde ele passa
nascem palavras
e frases

como frases
se fazem asas
palavras
o vento leve

o bicho alfabeto
passa
fica o que não se escreve

(from *La Vie in Close*, 1991)

The Animal Alphabet

The animal alphabet
has twenty-three paws
more or less

where it passes
words and phrases
are born

like phrases
wings are fashioned
words
the slight wind

the animal alphabet
passes
what one does not write remains

—*Translated from the Portuguese by Michael Palmer*

Duda Machado
1944

Born in Salvador, Bahia, Duda Machado majored in social sciences and literature, receiving a PhD in literature from the University of São Paulo.

During the 1970s he wrote popular lyrics for the early Tropicalist movement, and, while living in Rio de Janeiro, edited the avant-garde poetry review *Pólen.* Later, after moving to São Paulo, he published the magazines *Zil* (1977) and *Crescente* (1990). Today he makes his living from translation, having translated works by Gustave Flaubert, John Ashbery, and Allen Ginsberg.

VLADIMIR FONTES

Machado is the author of *Margem de uma ondo,* published by Editora 34 in 1997. He is currently Professor of Brazilian Literature at UFMG in the Minas Gerais State of Brazil.

BOOKS OF POETRY:

Margem de uma ondo (São Paulo: Editora 34, 1997)

147

Circunavegação

verbo que move o som
e outros sentidos

pacto
com o silêncio

colheita
de uma densa devastação

milimétrica medida
sopro súbito

monólogo
ao vento

manufraturada
flora de filamentos

fio que contém
seu próprio precipício

rio de todas as águas
a cada mergulho renascido

corpo-a-corpo
e inteira mente

(from *Margem de uma onda*, 1997)

Circumnavigation

verb that moves sound
and other senses

pact with silence

harvest
of a dense devastation

millimetric measure
sudden whisper

monologue
in the wind

manufractured
flora of filaments

thread that contains
its own precipice

river of all waters
at every dive revived

hand-to-hand
whole heartedly

—Translated from the Portuguese by Michael Palmer

Imagem de um Jardin

baque de pétalas
emudece o ar

jardim perfeito
onde se anula a tarde
jardim sem erro

jardim alheio
a qualquer idílio
ou atrocidade

(from *Margem de uma onda*, 1997)

Visão ao Avesso

neon insone
esquinas frigorífico
na madrugada
drogada
céu e asfalto
se ombreiam
exaustos
a uma canto
travesti e pivete
apressam um trato
:déjà vu
restos
pano rápido

(from *Margem de uma onda*, 1997)

The Image of a Garden

freefall of petals
hushes the air

perfect garden
where afternoon cancels itself
error-free garden

garden detached
from any idyll
or atrocity

—Translated from the Portuguese by Regina Alfarano

Inside-Out Vision

sleepless neon
icebox corners
in the drugged
dawn
sky and asphalt
exhausted
lean on each other
in the shadows
transvestite and street kid
strike a deal
:déjà vu
remnants
a quick rag

—Translated from the Portuguese by Dana Stevens

Álbum

velocidade
> de sóis
> árvores
> corpos

floração
> abrupta
> de agoras
> tão êxtase

manhãs
> atravessando

noites
na mesma
> frase-brisa

grãos
> arrebatados
> ao sal do mar
> dor dourada
> atordoada alegria

poros
> abertos
> ao ideal

canções
> que me adolescem
> e mentem

(from *Margem de uma onda*, 1997)

Album

speed

of suns
trees
bodies

blossoming

of nows
abrupt
such ecstasy

mornings

crossing
nights

along the same
breeze-phrase

grains

grasped
from the sea's salt
gilded grief
dazed gladness

pores

open
to the ideal

songs

that adolesce me
and lie

—Translated from the Portuguese by Regina Alfarano

Acontecimento

Para Augusto de Campos

qualquer,
algum ninguém

um outro
que
por sua vez

....

miragem
de reflexos espelhados

ponto
de interseção do real

foi

está escrito

(from *Margem de uma onda*, 1997)

Happening

for Augusto de Campos

anybody,
some nobody

someone else
who
in turn

. . . .

mirage
of mirrored reflections

point
of intersection of the real

it was

it is written

—*Translated from the Portuguese by Regina Alfarano*

Teatro Ambulante

Há três anos, representavam a mesma peça. O sucesso era tão grande e tantos os pedidos vindos de cidades do interior, que resolveram excursionar. Mas as viagens, ao contrário do que esperavam, iam acentuando ainda mais o cansaço e a rotina daquelas representações sempre idênticas. Para aliviar-se, os atores foram aumentando cada vez mais os trechos improvisados até que, pouco a pouco, a história e as personagens começaram a se alterar. Por fim, a peça se transformou. Mas a platéia não dava mostras de reparar naquela completa mudança. Ninguém reclamava e o público aceitava entusiasmado o outro drama representado e a presença daqueles atores famosos. Estes sentiam-se revigorados e o segredo da metamorfose atuava como um pacto a fortalecer a ligação entre eles.

Uma noite, passado algum tempo, sem que pudessem compreender ou controlar o que acontecia no palco, as palavras e os gestos que executavam, começaram a tornar-se alheios, irreconhecíveis. No segundo ato, todo o elenco estava assustado e atordoado. No entanto, no momento de cada réplica ou ação, o pânico desaparecia. Terminado o espetáculo, o público aplaudiu com o entusiasmo de sempre. Nos camarins, os atores mal conseguiam se entreolhar. Só mais tarde quando jantavam no restaurante do hotel, é que se sentiram capazes de reconhecer com excitação que haviam seguido diálogo por diálogo, cena por cena, a peça original, abandonada algum tempo atrás.

(from *Margem de uma onda,* 1997)

Traveling Theater

They had been performing the same play for three years. It was so successful, and the requests from country towns so many, that they decided to hit the road. Contrary to expectation, though, these trips only added to the exhaustion and routine of the always identical performances. By way of relief, the actors started improvising more and more until, little by little, the story and the characters began to change. In the end, the play underwent a transformation. But the audience did not seem to notice this complete change. No one complained and the spectators enthusiastically accepted the other play being performed, as well as the participation of such renowned actors, who felt reinvigorated. The secret metamorphosis acted like a pact to strengthen the liaison among them.

Some time had gone by when one night, unable to understand or control what took place on stage, the words uttered or the gestures made, the actors began to find each other strange, unrecognizable. By the second act, the whole cast was scared and bewildered. With each new line or action, though, the panic vanished. When the performance was over, the audience applauded as enthusiastically as always. In the dressing rooms, the actors could hardly look at each other. Only later, over dinner at the hotel restaurant, did they realize, with excitement, that they had followed every dialogue, every scene, from the original play abandoned some time back.

—*Translated from the Portuguese by Regina Alfarano, revised by Dana Stevens*

Almanaque

I

A matéria das estrelas
A primeira incógnita matemática

O que as ondas propagam
O mais leve dos átomos

A unidade das distâncias cósmicas
O corpo vegetativo das algas

O círculo que gira sobre si mesmo
A forma definitiva do inseto

O resultado da decomposição da luz
A temperatura do sangue nos reptéis

A função do nó
O que não é absoluto no ciclo

II

A forma da curva
O estado em que não há mais peso

Os condutos do sangue
A massa invisível do universo

A camada sob a crosta terrestre
O último ato do escorpião

Os olhos dos insetos
O ponto do céu acima do observador

A energia condensada
A vegetação das alturas

A curva quadrática
O fim do labirinto

(from *Margem de uma onda*, 1997)

Almanac

I

The matter of stars
The initial mathematical unknown

What waves propagate
The lightest of atoms

The unity of cosmic distances
The vegetal body of the algae

The circle that spins around itself
The insect's definitive shape

The result of light's decomposition
The temperature of blood in reptiles

The function of the knot
The nonabsolute in the cycle

II

The shape of the curve
The state in which there is no more weight

The ducts of the blood
The invisible mass of the universe

The layer beneath the earth's crust
The scorpion's final act

The eyes of insects
The point in the sky beyond the observer

Energy condensed
The vegetation on the heights

The quadratic curve
The end of the labyrinth

—*Translated from the Portuguese by Michael Palmer*

Antônio Moura
1964

Born in Belém in the Para State of the Amazon rain forest, Antônio Moura makes his living as an advertising writer, traveling between Belém and São Paulo. He has published two books of poetry to date, *Dez* and *Hong Kong e outros poemas.* His work has also been published in numerous magazines throughout Brazil, including *Cult* and the *Suplemento Literário de Minas Gerais.* He is now preparing a new book of poems to be published by Casa Fernando Pessoa in Lisbon, Portugal.

BOOKS OF POETRY:

Dez (Belém: Editora Supercores, 1997); *Hong Kong e outros poemas* (São Paulo: Ateliê, 1999).

ENGLISH LANGUAGE TRANSLATIONS:

Poems in "Lies About the Truth: An Anthology of Brazilian Poetry," edited by Régis Bonvicino in collaboration with Tarso M. de Melo, in *New American Writing*, no. 18 (2000).

Hong-Kong

A Edson e Fátima Secches

Paira
    sobre as cabeças
uma alta quantia de estrelas

Na terra
    olhos vendados
onde se lê grafitado: *à venda*

Sob
o céu
esticado
—tenda—
    o burburinho-mercado
prega
(pregão)
a milhõe$
     $
      $
   $
    $
$
de planetas

(nuvens com etiquetas)

à noite
    o sol é ouro especulado

(from *Hong-Kong & outros poems*, 1999)

Hong-Kong

for Edson and Fatima Secches

Hovers
    over heads
a large quantity of stars

On earth
    blindfolded eyes
where one reads grafittied: *for sale*

Above
the sky
stretched
—tent—
the clamoring market
nail
(proclaim)
the million$
      $
       $
   $
    $
$
of planets

(clouds with labels)

to the night
    the sun is speculated gold

—*Translated from the Portuguese by Jennifer Sarah Frota*

Mocambo

Meio-dia

olho-Sol
esbugalhado: Ó

os
so
retorcido: S
em brasa

sob a
pele sub
humana
esti — papiro — cada
seca sobre a carne zero
exposta ao
céu — miséria
a pino

Corpo — haste
ainda em riste

neste

cemi
tério-favela, semi
lírio

(from *Hong-Kong & outros poems*, 1999)

Hideout

Mid-day

solstice-ocular
ogle: Oh
os
sif
ied
twisted: S
smoldering

above the
skin sub
human
stre—papyrus—tched
dry above the zero flesh
exposed to the
sky—high
misery

Body—staff
unsheathed even

in this

ceme
tery—slum, semi
lilly

—Translated from the Portuguese by Jennifer Sarah Frota

Torquato Neto
1944-1972

Torquato Neto was born in Teresina, Piaui, in 1944. In 1972 he committed suicide in Rio de Janeiro.

One of the founders of the Tropicalist movement with Caetano Veloso and Gilberto Gil, Neto wrote the lyrics for "Geléia Geral," one of the key songs of the movement. His activities also included directing and acting in underground films. He co-edited the vanguard poetry journal *Navilouca* (1972). In the early 1970s, he wrote a column for the newspaper *Ultima Hora* in Rio de Janeiro. His only book of poetry, *Os últimos dias de paupéria*, was published posthumously, edited by Waly Salomão.

BOOKS OF POETRY:

Os últimos dias de paupéria (São Paulo: Max Limonad, 1982).

167

Cogito

eu sou como eu sou
pronome
pessoal intransferível
do homem que iniciei
na medida do impossível

eu sou como eu sou
agora
sem grandes segredos dantes
sem novos secretos dentes
nesta hora

eu sou como eu sou
presente
desferrolhado indecente
feito um pedaço de mim

eu sou como sou
vidente
e vivo tranquilamente
todas as horas do fim

(from *Os últimos dias de paupéria*, 1982)

Cogito

I am as I am
a pronoun
untransferable
from the man I began
at the measure of the impossible

I am as I am
now
without great secrets beneath
without new secret teeth
at this hour

I am as I am
present
unleashed, indecent
like a piece of myself

I am as I am
visionary
and I live peacefully
all the hours of the end

—*Translated from the Portuguese by Dana Stevens*

A Matéria o Material

3 estudos de som, para ritmo

arco
artefato
vivo
auriverde
sirv
o
a
fé
(ri?)
da fa
da, moça
in
feliz:

Matter Material

3 studies in sound, for rhythm

arch
artifact
living
greengold
i ser
ve
the
faith
(laugh?)
of the fair
y, un
happy
lady:

arco
art & fato
vi-vo
auriver-
te,
sir v
o
a fe
ri D
a fa
da (in)
feliz

                            : vivo(a) o -
                               crefoto
                              cr&ivo &
                                não/o
                          qui-Z
                                a   o
                                 rc
                                  o
                            auriver ...
                               te eu
                                sir
                                v.o.
                            § a raia-raiz

arch
art & fact
live ing
greengo-
l(a)dy
i serv
e
the (un)
happy
woun
de(a)d fair
y

           :living O-
           chrephoto
           I riddle &
           didn't wanT-
           o
           ar the
           ch
           the
           goldgreenY-
           ou I
           ser
           v.e.
           the roll-reel

```
a   o
  rc
  o
arte        fa-
            liz             &              vi-v.o.
                                           :
                                           auriv/ver
                                           te,
                                           rai
                                           Z


                                    paris, 29-7/2-8-69
```

(from *Os últimos dias de paupéria*, 1982)

the a
  r
  ch
  art

        fali-
        city   &   i li-v.e.
                                          :
                                          see-green/y
                                          ou
                                          roo
                                          T

paris, 7-29/ 8-2-69

—*Translated from the Portuguese by Michael Palmer*

Let's Play That

quando eu nasci
um anjo louco muito louco
veio ler a minha mão
não era um anjo barroco
era um anjo muito louco, torto
com asas de avião
eis que esse anjo me disse
apertando a minha mão
com um sorriso entre dentes
vai bicho desafinar
o coro dos contentes
vai bicho desafinar
o coro dos contentes
let's play that

musicada por Jards Macalé

(from *Os últimos dias de paupéria*, 1982)

você me chama
eu quero ir pro cinema
você reclama
e o meu amor não contenta
você me ama
mas de repente aquele trem já passou
faz quanto tempo
aquele tempo acabou

(from *Os últimos dias de paupéria*, 1982)

Let's Play That

when I was born
a crazy, very crazy angel
came to read my palm
it wasn't a baroque angel
it was a crazy, crooked angel
with wings like a plane
and behold, this angel told me,
pressing my hand
with a clenched smile:
go on, pal, sing off key
in the happy people's choir
go on, pal, sing off key
in the happy people's choir
let's play that

set to music by Jards Macalé

—Translated from the Portuguese by Dana Stevens

you call me up
I wanna go to the movies
you bawl me out
and my love doesn't please
you love me
but that train's already moved on
how much time
that time's been gone

—Translated from the Portuguese by Dana Stevens

Claudia Roquette-Pinto
1963

Claudia Roquette-Pinto was born in Rio de Janeiro in 1963. At the age of 17 she lived for seven months in San Francisco, completing a course in English and American Studies at San Francisco State University.

Back in Brazil, she worked in the fashion industry, first as a model and then as an assistant fashion producer. In 1987 she graduated from Pontifícia Universidade Católica in Literary Translation. From 1986 to 1991 she managed *Verve*, a monthly dedicated to literature and the arts, which she and four college friends had founded. She is the author of three books to date, *Os Dias Gagos, Saxífraga* and *Zona de sombra*, portions of which have appeared in the English translation *Shadow Zone.*

Roquette-Pinto lives with her husband and three children in Rio de Janeiro.

BOOKS OF POETRY:

Os Dias Gagos (author's edition, 1991); *Saxífraga* (Editora Salamandra, 1993); *Zona de sombra* (Rio de Janeiro: Sette Letras, 1997)

ENGLISH LANGUAGE TRANSLATIONS:

Shadow Zone (Los Angeles: Seeing Eye Books, 1999); selected poems in "Lies About the Truth: An Anthology of Brazilian Poety," edited by Régis Bonvicino in collaboration with Tarso M. de Melo, in *New American Writing*, no 18 (2000)

Minima Moralia

só a pétala mais rara
carna—
dura estriada
sem transparência de luz
só a pétala folheada
de água
onde mora (aguarda)
o som de uma floresta
pulsação dos fluidos da floresta
quando o tímpano estala

(from *Saxifraga*, 1993)

Castanhas, Mulheres

se abertas
com a destra surpresa
de pequenas mãos
cegas a tal alfabeto
e a nesga—já marron—
de pele fere
mais que a tolice dos espinhos
vê como
o gomo lateja:
ela e ela
desabotoa
entre os dedos

(from *Saxifraga*, 1993)

Minima Moralia

only the rarest petal
stri—
ated flesh
devoid of light's transparency
only the water-flecked
petal
wherein dwells (awaits)
the sound of a forest
the throbbing of a forest's fluids
when the eardrum crackles

—Translated from the Portuguese by Michael Palmer

Chestnuts, Women

if opened
with the surprising skill
of small hands
blind to such an alphabet
and if— itself brown—
the patch of skin bruises
even more than from foolish thorns
see how
the bud throbs:
she and she
unbuttons
between the fingers

—Translated from the Portuguese by Michael Palmer

Retrato de Pablo, Velho

da sombra seu rosto se lança
um peixe
uma lua africana
boiando à superfície gasta e gris
a calva não dava um aviso
dos olhos vivos
de água, vivos
que engendram antes de ver
a testa de touro tem brio
empurra um nariz repartido:
uma face enfrenta,
a outra subtrai
o resto são rugas e ricto
papiro
e o som de cascos ancestrais

(from *Saxifraga*, 1993)

Vão

palavra como persiana
poema como lucidez
imanta o ar fora do cômodo
das frases   um outono
rente à janela
ouro tonto sobre a tarde derrubada
entrementes, entre dentes
(e quatro paredes)
tua boca ainda invoca
equívoca e pobre.
na penugem além da vidraça
os deuses-de-tudo-o-que-importa
cerram as pálpebras de cobre

(from *Zona de sombra*, 1997)

Portrait of Pablo, Agèd

from the shadow his face hurls itself forth
a fish
an african moon
floating above the worn and grey surface
the bald spot gave no hint
of the eyes lively
as water, so lively
they create before seeing
the prideful bull's brow
thrusts a split nose:
one side of the face confronts
the other withdraws
the rest is wrinkles and grimace
papyrus
and the sound of ancestral hooves

—Translated from the Portuguese by Michael Palmer

In Vain

word like window blind
poem like lucidity
magnetizes the air outside the room
of phrases   autumn
near the pane
dizzy gold over demolished afternoon
between minutes, between teeth,
(and four walls)
your mouth still summoning
equivocal and faint.
in the shutter beyond the glass
the gods-of-everything-that-matters
close copper eyelids

—Translated from the Portuguese by Michael Palmer

No Éden

peça a ela que se desnude
começa pelos cílios
segue-se ao arame dos
utensílios diários
insônia alinhavando-se
de tiros,
a infância   seus disfarces
é preciso
que se arranque toda a face
deixar que os olhos descansem
lado a lado com os sapatos
na camurça oscilante
de um quarto
isso, se quer (sequer desconfia)
tocar o que se fia (um par
de presas, topázios)
entre os vãos das costelas
abra o fecho ela desfecha
no escuro o quandrante onde vaza
a luz e suas arestas

(from *Zona de sombra*, 1997)

In Eden

ask her to undress
begin with the eyelashes
followed by the wire of
daily utensils
(insomnia alleviating itself
of shots,
childhood   its disguises)
it's necessary
to strip the entire face
to rest the eyes
side by side with the shoes
in the oscillating suede
of a bedroom
this, if you wish (even if you distrust)
to touch what one trusts (a pair
of prey, topazes)
between the rib's voids
opens the closure she discloses
in the dark the quadrant where
the light and her edges
spill

—*Translated from the Portuguese by Jennifer Sarah Frota*

Waly Salomão
1944

Born in Jequié, Bahia, in 1944, Waly Salomão gradu-
ated from law school, but never worked as an attor-
ney. A poet, lyricist, and promoter of cultural events,
Salomão has lived in Rio de Janeiro for many years.
    Among his publications are *Me segura qu'eu vou
dar um troço* (prose, 1972). *Gigolô de bibelô* (prose
and poetry, 1983), and *Armarinho de Miudezas* (criti-
cism, prose and poetry, 1993). Most recently he pub-
lished *Algaravias/Câmara de Ecos* (1996). With
Torquato Neto, he edited the single-issue journal
Navilouca (1971-1974). He also wrote lyrics for sev-
eral musicians, among them Caetano Veloso, Jards
Matcalé and João Bosco. Salomão is one of the per-
manent curators for the collection of the Brazilian artist Hélio Oiticica.

JANETE LONGO

BOOKS OF POETRY:

Gigolô de bibelô; *Armarinho de Miudezas*; *Algaravias/Câmara de Ecos* (Rio de Janeiro: Editora
34, 1996).

Minha Alegria

minha alegria permanece eternidades soterrada
e só sobe para a superfície
através dos tubos de filtros alquímicos e não da causalidade natural.
ela é filha bastarda do desvio e da desgraça,
minha alegria: um diamante gerado pela combustão,
como rescaldo final de incêndio.

(from *Algaravias/Câmara de Ecos*, 1996)

My Joy

My joy spends eternities buried
and only rises to the surface
through tubes of alchemical filters, not by natural causes.
She is the bastard daughter of waywardness and disgrace,
my joy: a diamond generated by combustion,
like the smoldering remains of an inferno.

—Translated from the Portuguese by Dana Stevens

Meia-Estação

Presságios nas flores abertas dos junquilhos;
                              abertas, justamente, hoje de manhã.
O arco-íris e seu sortilégio,
                              justamente, hoje de manhã.
Folhas de figueiras levitantes, aéreas.
A baba epiléptica do mar hermafrodita:
                    macho lambendo a areia da praia arreganhada;
                    fêmea singrada por navios duros,
                                        de ferros e aços,
                    e seu mostruário-monstruário de mastros.
Tarda a vir o outono este ano,
                    o verão não quer se despedir.
Um vento quente passa e acorda
                    os feitiços e as promessas do verão inteiro.
Escrever assim é romantizar o vento quente que passa
                              a lembrar somente
que é o vento quente e desaforado
a passar uma lixa grossa
sobre a cidade, os seres e as coisas.

Vento bêbado de amnésia e desmemória,
incapaz de verão ou outono ter por nome próprio,
trafega indiferente à nossa tradição ibérica
que exige para tudo registro e certidão,
pagamento de estampilha ou selo do tesouro,
aval e avalista,
                    reconhecimento de firma
                                        por tabelião em cartório.
Além do estilo—imperativo categórico—do nosso arquétipo
                              de tabelião perfunctório

        (parente lusitano-brasileiro do literalista pedante de Miss
Marianne Moore)

                                        cujo breviário reza:

"Lavro e dou fé … é verão."
Ou
"Lavro e dou fé … é outono."

(from *Algaravias/Câmara de Ecos*, 1996)

Half-Season

Auguries in the jonquil flowers;
                                        opened, precisely, this morning.
The rainbow and its witchcraft,
                                        precisely, this morning.
Fig-tree leaves levitating, airborne.
The epileptic drool of a hermaphrodite sea:
                        the male licking the split sand of the beach;
                        the female navigated by hard boats,
                                        by iron and steel,
                        and the monster-masters of masts.
Autumn is late this year,
                        summer won't say goodbye.
A warm wind passes and wakens
                        the spells and promises of an entire summer.
To write this way is to romanticize the warm wind that passes
                        remembering only
that it is the warm and insolent wind
dragging rough sandpaper
across the city, its beings and things.

A wind drunk with amnesia and unremembering,
unnameable either as summer or autumn,
traverses indifferently our Iberian tradition,
which insists that everything be registered, certified,
stamped or sealed by the treasury,
bond and bondsman,
                        the firm's recognition
                                in the office of a notary public.
Not to mention the style—a categorical imperative—of our
        archetype of the perfunctory office

                (a Luso-Brazilian relation of Miss
Marianne Moore's pedant literalist)

                        whose breviary prays:

"I hereby bear witness… it's summer."
Or
"I hereby bear witness … it's autumn."

        —*Translated from the Portuguese by Dana Stevens*

Domingo de Ramos

I

O indesejado das gentes entrou, enfim, na cidade.
Seu peito é só cavidade e espinho encravado,
cacto do deserto das cercanias,
torpor de quem se sente aplicado por cicuta
ou mordido de cobra.

O que, convenhamos, lhe dá um ar desapegado

                        das coisas triviais

e acresce seu charme

            paradoxal

                 perante o populacho.

A cidade é uma nebulosa de sonho:
tempos e lugares diversos embaralhados,
tantas glórias e hosanas, tantos pedidos de empregos,
partidos, facções, crimes organizados, júbilos e adulações.

Uma sensação de déjà vu

            que murcha qualquer frescor

                 na idade madura.

Palm Sunday

I

He, the least wanted by all, has finally entered the city.
His chest is nothing but cavity and embedded thorns,
desert cactus of the outskirts,
torpor of one who feels drugged by hemlock
or snakebite.

Which, we agree, lends him a detached air
　　　　　　　　　　　　　　　　　　from trivial things
and adds to his paradoxical
　　　　　　　　　　charm

　　　　　　　　　　　　　　in the eyes of the populace.
The city nebulous like a dream:
various times and places jumbled up,
so many glories and hosannas, so many requests for jobs,
parties, factions, organized crime, jubilees, adulations.

A sensation of déjà vu
　　　　　　　　　withering any freshness
　　　　　　　　　　　in its ripe age.

　　　　　　　　　　　　　•

II

Assim falava o antecessor:
"O poeta é um ressentido e o mais são nuvens."
Assim ele, aqui, fala:
Os ressentimentos esfiapados
       são como nuvens esgarçadas.

Campo aberto,
ele vira uma câmara de ecos.
Câmara de ecos:
a substância do próprio tutano tornada citação.

Aprende a palidez altiva
e sorriso aloof
de quem comprende as variações dos ventos da mídia.
Estas qualidades ele supõe ter importado de Stendhal
e de Emerson,
já de Drummond ele assimila uma certa qualidade esconsa,
retalho daqui, recorte dali,
etcetera et caterva.

Ele: o amalgâmico
      o filho das fusões
           o amante das algaravias
o sem pureza.

Como compor, com semelhante *melting pot*,
uma inteireza de homem
que caiba no anúncio "Ecce Homo"?

II

Here's how the antecedent spoke:
"The poet is resentful and the rest are clouds."
This is how he speaks here:
Frayed resentments
                                   are like shredded clouds.

Open field,
he becomes an echo-chamber.
Echo-chamber:
the essence of the marrow itself has become quotation.

He learns the lofty pallor
and aloof smile
of one who understands the media's fickle winds.
These qualities he believes borrowed from Stendhal
and Emerson,
while from Drummond he draws a certain obliqueness,
a morsel here, a snippet there,
et cetera et caterva.

He: the amalgamated
                          the son of fusions
                                        the lover of gibberish
the impure.

How to compose, with such a melting pot,
the entirety of a man
to fit the billing "Ecce Homo"?

III

Hoje é
Palm Sunday,
uma boa oportunidade para sobrevoar
de helicóptero:

os manguezais de esgotos negros e garças brancas,
os morros
de parcas palmas de palmeiras
e muito capim colonião
—o capim colonião ao vento parece uma cabeleira
encharcada de gel—
as praias
onde E L E simula
                              —através das leis do Livro do Caos—
o delírio demiúrgico
de que as hélices do helicóptero são as provocadoras
                                        das ondas do mar.

Palm Sunday.
Dentro do helicóptero
                        lá em cima
o diabo recorda-lhe, então, um conto de Sartre,
sobre Erostrato, o piromaníaco,
que adorava olhar os homens
bem do alto
como se fossem
formiguinhas.

(from *Algaravias/Câmara de Ecos*, 1996)

III

Today is
Palm Sunday,
a good opportunity to fly over
by helicopter:

the mango groves with black gutters and white herons
the hills
the parched palms of palm-trees
and lots of crabgrass
—the crabgrass in the wind is like hair
soaked in gel—
the beaches
where H E fakes
                              —through the laws of the Book of Chaos—
the demiurgical delirium
that the helicopter's blades are what provokes
the ocean's waves.

Palm Sunday.
Inside the helicopter
                              there on high
the devil then reminds him of a story by Sartre,
about Erostratus, the pyromaniac,
who loved to watch men
from way up high:
they looked like
tiny ants.

   —Translated from the Portuguese by Dana Stevens

Federico Tavares Bastos Barbosa
1961

Born in Recife, Pernambuco, on February 20, 1961, Federico Tavares Bastos Barbosa moved to São Paulo when he was six. Barbosa began undergraduate studies in physics and Greek, which he never concluded, though he did major in Portuguese language and literature. A literary critic at *Jornal da Tarde* and *Folha de S. Paulo* for some time, he currently teaches Brazilian and Portuguese literature courses. His poems have been published in various journals in Brazil. His books include *Rarefato* (1990) and *Nada Feito Nada* (1993).

BOOKS OF POETRY:

Rarefato (São Paulo: Iluminuras, 1990); *Nana Feito Nada* (São Paulo: Editorial Perspectiva, 1993); *Contra-corrente* (São Paulo: Iluminuras, 2000)

Lascaux 1986

no cinema de Lascaux
(imagem sobre imagem)
cortes:
séculos de Klee

recortes de cores
nos desenhos do Kane
na voz bellae
(Billie & Ella)
nas suas pernas cruzadas
em frente à tv

mágico quase acaso
colorindo
(como que sem querer)
a caverna escura
em que a gente se vê

(from *Rarefato*, 1990)

Rarefato

Nenhuma voz humana aqui se pronuncia
chove um fantasma anárquico, demolidor

amplo nada no vazio deste deserto
anuncia-se como ausência, carne em unha

odor silencioso no vento escarpa
corte de um espectro pousando na água

tudo que escoa em silêncio em tempo ecoa

(from *Rarefato*, 1990)

Lascaux 1986

at the Cinema Lascaux
(image over image)
cuts:
centuries of Klee

cross-sections of colors
in the drawings of Kane
in the bellae voice
(Billie & Ella)
in her crossed legs
in front of the TV

chance-like magic
coloring
as if by accident
the dark cavern
in which we find ourselves

—*Translated from the Portuguese by Michael Palmer*

Rarefactus

No human voice   here   speaks out
an anarchic phantom pours,   demolisher

full nothing in the emptiness of this desert
offers itself as absence,   nail flesh

silent scent in the wind   slope
spectre's cross-section   at rest   in the water

all that in silence flows in due time echoes

—*Translated from the Portuguese by Michael Palmer*

Josely Vianna Baptista
1957

Born in Curitiba in 1957, Josely Vianna Baptista began translating works of fiction, poetry, and essays in the mid 1980s. She has translated into Portuguese some of the most important writers in Spanish, including Alejo Carpentier, Cabrera Infante, Julio Cortázar, Severo Sarduy, Mario Vargas Llosa, Juan Goytisolo, Nestor Perlonguer, José Lezama Lima and others. For the publisher Editorial Aldus in México, she edited an anthology of Brazilian poetry in 2001, which included many of the figures in this volume, among them Paulo Leminski, Waly Salomão, Arnaldo Antunes, Carlito Azevedo and Régis Bonvicino.

As a poet, she published *Ar* in 1991 and *Corpografia* in 1992. More recently, she has worked with visual artist Francisco Faria for a visual-poetic installation for the 5th Biennal in Havana (1994). Two new books will be published in 2001, *De zero ao zênite* and *Sol sobre nuvens*, the later of which will be published by Editora Perspectiva in São Paulo.

BOOKS OF POETRY:

Ar (São Paulo: Iluminuras, 1991); *Corpografia* (São Paulo: Iluminuras, 1992)

ENGLISH LANGUAGE TRANSLATIONS:

Poems in "Lies About the Truth: An Anthology of Brazilian Poetry," edited by Régis Bonvicino in collaboration with Tarso M. de Melo, in *New American Writing*, no 18 (2000).

Os Poros Flóridos

Fim de tarde, as sombras suam
sua tintura sobre as cores, extraem
da fava rara da luz o contorno das coisas,
as rugas na concha de um molusco,
grafismos, vieiras milenares com reservas
de sal, poema estranho trançado
em esgarços de oleandros,
enquanto corpos
mergulham em câmara lenta,
e nada é imagem
(teu corpo branco em mar de sargaços),
nada é miragem
na tela rútila das pálpebras.

(previously unpublished)

Um Som de Antigas Águas Apagadas.

... miragem a rima, a fábula do nada,
as falhas dessa fala em desgeografia,
a fala hermafrodita, imantação de astilhas,
a voz na transparência, edifícios de areia.

Mas teu olhar o mesmo, em íris-diafragma,
fotogramas a menos na edição do livro,
e o enredo sonho e sol, delírios insulares,
teu olhar transparente, a imagem
margem d'água, e as fábulas da fala,
as falhas desse nada—superfície de alvura

ou árida escritura.

Na moldura da página,
marginália de escarpas.

(previously unpublished)

Florid Pores

Late afternoon, the shadows spill
their tints over colors, extract
the contour of things from the light's odd grain,
the grooves on a mollusk shell,
tracings, millenary scallops with salt
deposits, strange poem woven
among shreds of oleander
while bodies
dive in slow motion
and nothing is image
(your white body engulfed in seaweed)
nothing is mirage
on the eyelids' shining screen.

—*Translated from the Portuguese by Michael Palmer*

A Sound of Ancient, Faded Flows

...the rhyme is a mirage, fable of nothingness,
   the flaws of speech deterritorialized,
hermaphroditic speech, splinters magnetized,
voice through transparency, buildings of sand.

But your gaze the same, an iris-diaphragm,
   photograms missing from the published book,
the sun and dream plot and insular deliriums,
   your transparent gaze, the image
water's edge, and the fables of speech,
the flaws of such nothingness—a surface of whitness

            or arid scribblings.

At page's border,
marginalia of slopes.

—*Translated from the Portuguese by Michael Palmer*

Infinitis

para nietzsche

entre   bétulas   e   nadas,   nadas
e   madrugadas,   beats,   fadas,   f
ugas,   árias,   entre   gélidas   p
étalas   de   neve,   leves   crista
is   limando   *nichts*   de   fumaça
,   entre   picos   e   abismos,   bét
ulas   e   nadas,   lá,   onde   o   ar
falta: ali   sua   fala   limalha
polindo   tudo   e   um   isso: no   c
repúsculo   dos   ídolos,   divino   s
idos   (andarilho   entre   verd
ades   e   mentiras),   à   procura   da
flor   que   brota,   rara   na   rocha,
entre   *neins*   e   pistilos,   aurora
,   pedra   lascada: na   alta
engadina   valquírias   cav   algam
luas   que   ainda   uivam   para
lous,   e   o   visionário,   no
limiar,   parindo   centauros

(from *Ar*, 1991)

Infinites

for nietzsche

between birches and nothing
s, nothings and dawns, beat
s, fairies, fugues, arias, am
ong frozen snow petals, lig
ht crystals polishing *nichts*
of smoke, among peaks and
abysses, birches and nothin
gs, there, where there's no
air: there your sandy speech
polishing everything, and a
this: at the sunset of the
idols, once divine (wanderer
among truths and lies)
searching for the blooming
flower, rare on the rock,
among neins and pistils,
aurora, hewn stone: on the
high engadine walkyries
ride on moons that still
howl to lous, and the
visionary, on the threshold,
giving birth to centaurs

—*Translated from the Portuguese by Regina Alfarano*

na   madrugada   fria   a   pai
sagem   se   vê   através   da   p
aisagem,a   geada   e   a   lasc
a   de   um   jaspe   que   se   par
ece   ao   jade,as   gazes   da   g
eada   que   esfumam   a   pais
agem,   e   a   lasca   de   um   j
aspe   que   se   parece   ao   ja
de   e   se   repete   jaspe   na
geada   paisagem,   na   casc
a   de   áspide   ,   na   valsa
de   uma   vespa,   no   rasgo
de   um   outdoor,   na   aura   d
e   um   poema,   na   mineral   f
umaça   da   boca   de   quem
fala,   no   ar   em   ar   a
r s   que   condensa   uma   im
agem,geada,   jade,   jaspe   n
a   pele   da   paisagem,   q   ue
o   áspero   da   espera   alter   a
em   miragem: formigas   t
raçam   trilhas   na   farinha

(from *Ar*, 1991)

in   cold   dawn,   landscape   is   seen
through   other   landscape,   white   frost
and   jasper   sliver   that   looks   like
jade,   with   frost   gauzes   shading   the
hazy   landscape   ,   and   the   jasper   sliver
that   looks   like   jade   and   repeats
itself   in   the   frost   landscape,   in   the
skin   of   an   asp   ,   in   the   waltz   of   a
wasp   ,in   the   slit   of   a   billboard   ,   in
the   aura   of   a   poem,   in   the   mineral
smoke   from   one   whispering   mouth   ,   in
the   air   in   to   air   into   *ars*   that
condense   an   image,   white   frost,   and
geode,   and   jade   ,   and   jasper   on   the
face   of   this   landscape,   and   changed
into   a   mirage   by   asperities   of
waiting:some   ants   are   tracing   tracks
in flour

—*Translated from the Portuguese by Regina Alfarano*

u m d i a e u f ó r i c a
o u t r o s p o r f o r a
u m d i a e n g a g é e
o u t r o r e t o m b é e
a p u r o u m d i a
o u t r o r i g o r e o
d i a u r z e s e
a l c a ç u z e s v e z e s
q u e b r u x a o
u t r a s q u e m u s a s e
u m d i a b l a n c o o s
o u t r o s s a l v o s
u m d i a d e s f e i t a
o u t r o s p e r f e i t a u m
o u t r o e m d i a u m
d i a u m o u t r o d i a
s e m d n e m v o c ê

(from *Corpografia*, 1992)

one day euphoric other
stratospheric one day
engagée another
retombée if plight one
day rigor another and
the day heather and
licorice at times a
witch others a muse if
one day blanco others
saved if one day right
others savaged one up
to date one day
another day with-out
' d ' without thee

—*Translated from the Portuguese by Regina Alfarano*

```
g r a a l        e m        v i l a        v e l h a        o u        n a        p
o n t e            v e c c h i o ,          n a s            l a j e s          l i m
a d a s          p e l o s          g r ã o s        d e        a r e i a ,        n
a        l i s t r a        r i s c a d a        e n t r e          p e d
r a        e        l í q u e n        ,        a r e s t a s        d e        j a
d e ,        c r i s t a s        d e        g r a n i t o ,        e m        i
l h a s          d e          m i n a s ,          n e b u l o s i d a d
e s ,          n a s          m a r g e n s          t r a n q u i l a
s        q u e        o        g r a n i z o        f r i s a        ,        n u
m        f r e m i r        d e        l á b i o s ,        r e t i n i
r        d e        d e n t e s        ,        n a        t u a        a l e g r i
a        o u        n o        s e n s o        e m        d e s l i z e        d
o s          o l h o s          e m          f a l s o          d e s c o b r
i n d o          o c e l o s          n a s          a s a s          e s t r i a
d a s          d e          u m          p e q u e n o
i n s e t o
```

((from *Corpografia*, 1992)

grail   at   villa   velha   or   ponte
vecchio,   on   slabs   sanded   by
tiny   sand   grains,in   the   ledge   d
rawn   between   the   rock   and
lichens,   and   jade   edges,   granite
crests,in   island   mines,   neb
ulosities,   on   the   tranquil
margins   which   hail   crisps   ,   in
the   quivering   of   lips,   ringing   of
teeth,   in   your   happiness   or   in
the   sliding   sense   of   misled   eyes
sighting   ocelli   in   the   f   luted
wings   of   a   little   insect

—*Translated from the Portuguese by Regina Alfarano*

INDEX OF VOLUMES 1-3

GREEN INTEGER
Pataphysics and Pedantry

Douglas Messerli, *Publisher*

Essays, Manifestos, Statements, Speeches, Maxims,
Epistles, Diaristic Notes, Narratives, Natural Histories,
Poems, Plays, Performances, Ramblings, Revelations
and all such ephemera as may appear necessary
to bring society into a slight tremolo of confusion
and fright at least.

*

Green Integer Books